Slaves of Christ

Slaves of Christ

*A First-Century Understanding
for Twenty-First-Century Christians*

ROBERT GADEKEN

WIPF & STOCK · Eugene, Oregon

SLAVES OF CHRIST
A First-Century Understanding for Twenty-First-Century Christians

Copyright © 2025 Robert Gadeken. All rights reserved. Except for brief quotations in critical publications or reviews, no part of this book may be reproduced in any manner without prior written permission from the publisher. Write: Permissions, Wipf and Stock Publishers, 199 W. 8th Ave., Suite 3, Eugene, OR 97401.

Wipf & Stock
An Imprint of Wipf and Stock Publishers
199 W. 8th Ave., Suite 3
Eugene, OR 97401

www.wipfandstock.com

PAPERBACK ISBN: 979-8-3852-4151-4
HARDCOVER ISBN: 979-8-3852-4152-1
EBOOK ISBN: 979-8-3852-4153-8

Unless otherwise indicated, Scripture quotations are from the ESV® Bible (The Holy Bible, English Standard Version®), copyright ©2001 by Crossway Bibles, a publishing ministry of Good News Publishers. Used by permission. All rights reserved.

Scripture quotations marked (NIV) are taken from the Holy Bible, New International Version®, NIV®. Copyright © 1973, 1978, 1984, 2011 by Biblica, Inc.® Used by permission of Zondervan. All rights reserved worldwide. www.zondervan.com The "NIV" and "New International Version" are trademarks registered in the United States Patent and Trademark Office by Biblica, Inc.®

To Cheryl

I lift up my eyes to you,
to you who sit enthroned in heaven.
As the eyes of slaves look to the hand of their master,
as the eyes of a female slave look to the hand of her mistress,
so our eyes look to the Lord our God,
till he shows us his mercy.

— Psalm 123:1–2 (NIV)

Contents

Introduction 1

PART 1: SOME "ISSUES"
Chapter 1: The Problem of Obedience 13
Chapter 2: Isn't "Slave" Just a Metaphor? 30
Chapter 3: How Can Slavery Be a Good Thing? 45
Takeaway 69

PART 2: BELONGING
Chapter 4: What Does It Mean to Belong? 73
Chapter 5: Born a Slave 94
Chapter 6: The Marks of a Slave 101
Takeaway 107

PART 3: SERVING
Chapter 7: Work or Service? 111
Chapter 8: What Does Service Look Like? 129
Takeaway 148

PART 4: BRINGING IT ALL TOGETHER
Chapter 9: "Something Better" 153

Bibliography 163

Introduction

"You have been set free from sin and have become slaves of God."
—Romans 6:22

"A slave of Christ" was one of the ways the first Christians described themselves (Rom 1:1; Jas 1:1; 2 Pet 1:1). Jesus told them that "whoever would be first among you must be your slave, even as the Son of Man came not to be served but to serve, and to give his life as a ransom for many" (Matt 20:27–28). And on the night he was betrayed, he acted like a slave and washed his disciples' feet, saying that this was an example of how they should serve each other (John 13:12–17). And so, this was simply how the early Christians understood themselves. The editor of the *Journal of Early Christian History* has written: "The metaphor of slavery was probably one of the most influential and, at the same time, pervasive forms of speech to seize early Christian discourse. It can be well argued that no other metaphor was as dominant in the formation of early Christian theology and ethics."[1] I believe it is time for us to claim this identity once more—but not as a metaphor.

I believe that Paul, James, Peter, and all the early Christians understood this in a very literal way. They belonged to Jesus and served him just as slaves in their time would serve a human master, only he wasn't a human master. And that made all the difference. He was God, their creator, redeemer, and rightful master, and this transformed the evil and idolatrous human institution into something that could be used to reflect the Bible's understanding of creator/creature, father/family, master/disciple, and especially Savior/saved. As Luther would put it in his famous explanation of the second article of the Apostle's Creed: "He purchased and won me . . . that I

---

1. de Wet, *Preaching Bondage*, 46.

may be his own . . . live under him in his kingdom and serve him."[2] This is the very definition of a slave.

I will consider "slave of Christ" not as a metaphor of commitment, which seems to be our modern view, but as a definition of what it means to be a Christian—our identity—who we are and how this determines what we do. As Chris de Wet has said, slavery was a tool to "think with" in the first century, defining a whole system of relationships in that world.[3] This view of slavery can be a "tool to think with" for us as well that can help us to understand and adapt to our own time. This will require a careful comparison of contexts, both from the first century and from our own time. This is not nostalgia. It was a brutal age, and no one would advocate turning back the clock. There were, however, some valuable lessons that have been lost along the way and are worth going back to find. I think "slave of Christ" is one of them.

What exactly does it mean to be a slave of Christ? With a two-thousand-year distance from that time and that culture, with all the various forms of slavery since and all the history of man's struggle for freedom and democracy in the Western world, our understanding of those words has changed. Oh, we recognize those words, and we may think we know what they mean, but the context has shifted, and the meanings of words change. We may think, for example, that we can simply replace that negative word "slavery" with "servant"—but they were not, and are not, the same. We may think the image of slavery outdated, insulting and unhelpful—but what if it is has something to teach us? Perhaps it is the way we understand that word in our time and place that is unhelpful. But curiously, the idea from that time and place may be more helpful now than ever before, both in understanding who we are, in our identity and our calling, and in our witness to the modern world.

Consider, for example, that twenty-first-century Christians now share something very significant with first-century Christians. Christians are once more a small minority in a religiously pluralistic civilization that looks on them with suspicion, if not hostility. Although it is true that in recent surveys something like 60 percent of Americans still identify as Christian, the actual number of Christians who would confess a faith resembling the traditional creeds is probably closer to half that, perhaps less than one in

---

2. Luther, *Luther's Small Catechism*, 17.
3. de Wet, *Unbound God*, 6–9.

Introduction

three Americans.⁴ And those Christians whose lives look different from non-Christians in their morality, priorities, marriages, and families are no doubt even fewer than that. Yet America is still considered more "Christian" than most other Western countries.

This brings us to one more important thing we Christians share with first century Christians—bad press. Being a Christian used to be considered a good thing—well, no longer. Christians are now considered judgmental, narrow-minded, arrogant people who talk about love but never show it. We are said to hate people who are different from us and are always telling others how to live. We are said to have a political agenda to deny women, homosexuals, and transgender people their rights. Christians are now considered dangerous people who should be controlled and restricted as much as possible.

Thankfully, most Christians are not anything like this negative caricature. Like their first-century counterparts, they are often misunderstood and maligned. In the first century, Christians were thought to be cannibals because they ate someone's body and blood; incestuous because Christian "brothers" married their Christian "sisters"; and atheists because they didn't worship an idol in a temple, i.e., "the real gods." And because they didn't worship the accepted idols, people believed these gods were angry at being ignored and would then bring punishment on everyone. In that case, any bad thing that happened could be blamed on the Christians and so justify the persecution they often received. The modern misunderstandings of Christianity may not be for quite the same reasons, but the response of suspicion, anger, and persecution is the same.

Though there are some who dislike Christianity for very specific reasons, most, as in the ancient world, are only acting on rumors out of ignorance. All many people know of Christianity is what they've seen in the media or what their teachers in school, popular celebrities, and political leaders have told them. They don't really know any Christians, at least not any who will talk to them about what they believe and why. Nor can they recognize Christians by the way they act, because most American Christians do not act any differently than people in the culture around them. It's the "strange ones" who make it on TV, not those who humbly seek to follow Jesus—and these last are apparently not talking.

There is, of course, great irony here. There is an adage that says whatever someone criticizes in others is probably the very thing they are guilty

---

4. Burge, *Nones*, 15–23; Barna, "American Worldview Inventory," 2–3.

of themselves. The vocal critics of Christianity seem to be far more judgmental, narrow-minded, and arrogant than the worst Christian offenders. These critics seem to hate those who think differently. They seem to have a political agenda to deny Christians their rights. On the other hand, they want to enforce a "politically correct" agenda, telling others how they should live. My point, however, is not whether this is fair but simply that many people actually believe what these critics say about Christians. In our time and place, just as in the first century, Christians are simply not considered "normal."

How did Christians in the first century respond to a world that considered them strange, and perhaps even dangerous? They engaged with those around them. The well-educated among them wrote many works in defense of what Christians believed, and they spoke in the forums and assemblies to defend it. But most Christians then, as now, were not the well-educated writers and speakers. Yet they were the ones who did the best work of defending and spreading their faith because they lived as slaves of Christ in their normal occupations. They worked with, made friends with, and served those who did not understand them. Since they could perhaps be killed for this faith, they made sure they understood it well and would be found faithful and obedient to Jesus. Their lives looked different from those around them, and they were willing to explain their hope to all (1 Pet 3:14–16). They firmly believed that they belonged to Jesus and, even at the cost of their lives, they wanted to please him and live with him eternally.

In all this, it helped them greatly to identify with the label "slaves of Christ." As Paul wrote, they had been "bought at a price" by the blood of Jesus, and now they served him in their daily lives, no matter how strange their actions appeared to others or how people reacted to their words. Because "slave of Christ" defined them, it determined how they thought of themselves and how they lived. Because they lived and worked side by side with pagans, their lives (and sometimes their deaths) eventually changed many of their enemies into friends and some into faithful followers of Jesus. This is not only how they survived but how the early church grew.[5]

What Is a Christian?

At this point, we should probably say something about the terms you will find in this book. "Church-speak" that uses words like "sin," "repentance,"

---

5. Green, *Evangelism in the Early Church*, 180–85, 235.

Introduction

"absolution," "sanctification," and "grace" is almost a foreign language because it is never heard outside of church. The words "church" and "Christianity" are especially misunderstood. If you say "church," most people think you mean an organization that you join, like a political party (an especially common comparison in the minds of non-Christians). As an organization, it works for a cause, and it serves its members by providing a local "clubhouse" for worship (a "pep rally for the cause") with "preaching" (telling you what to think and how to act) and offering you morale-building ceremonies (like baptism and communion). Sadly, many think the cause of Christianity is moral perfection and working for the moral perfection of others. Naturally, then, everyone in the church is a hypocrite because they aren't any better than anyone else. So, from this point of view, a Christian is someone who goes to church and thinks they are better than everyone else, and their main goal is to get everybody else to go to church and be perfect hypocrites too.

The Bible understands the church very differently. In fact, biblically speaking, you can't "go to church," because a church is not a place. The word in the New Testament is *ekklesia*, from *kaleo*, "to call," and means "a group of people who have been called together." In fact, Christians can be referred to simply as "the called" (1 Cor 1:24). They are not just called into a meeting but into a faith relationship with Jesus, and into a relationship with each other.

Perhaps a better translation of *ekklesia* than simply an "assembly" might be as in the Apostles' Creed: "a communion of saints." In popular understanding, a saint is a very good person or even a perfect person, but according to the Bible, there are only two ways someone can be holy: never do anything wrong or be forgiven. It is only the second that makes one a Christian and a part of the Christian church. When you put your faith in Jesus, you receive the forgiveness of your sin won by his cross, and, in that way, you and other Christians become without sin or "holy ones," or in Latin, "saints." Paul describes the church this way: "To the church of God that is in Corinth, to those sanctified in Christ Jesus, called to be saints together with all those who in every place call upon the name of our Lord Jesus Christ, both their Lord and ours" (1 Cor 1:2).

We are saints because of what Jesus did on a cross to take away our sin. We are a communion of saints because those who are called to faith in Jesus are, at the same time, called into a fellowship of people. It is one call. When you respond to God's call to put your faith and hope in Jesus, you not only belong to Jesus but also to everyone else who belongs to Jesus. As in math, two things equal to the same thing are equal to each other. We serve Jesus by serving them (1 Cor 12:7) and those around us in the world. More than a math fact, however, we become part of an organism, the body of Christ, not an organization (1 Cor 12).

In Scripture, you cannot "go" to church, but you can "be" the church, assembled with your fellow "slaves" so that Christ, your head and master, can teach and strengthen you with his word and sacrament, and with the encouragement from others. And all this so that you will not only be faithful and obedient to Jesus in your life but also help others respond to God's call and follow Jesus as his forgiven people into eternal life. Slaves of Christ make slaves of Christ by being the church in the world—this is what is meant by the term "Christianity." It is not a moral or social cause, political movement, philosophy, or organization. It is who we are, or as some would say it, "whose" we are.

Many people rightfully mistrust organizations because of the ease with which they can be taken over and controlled by their leaders. But biblically, the only head of the church is Jesus, and he rules us with his word. The church consists of those who listen to the master's voice and follow him (John 10:27–28). But since the church is made up of people, it can be managed as if it were an organization of people, with strong leaders controlling it. When the leaders of a church do not teach God's word but invent new laws or standards for believers that are not found in God's word, it is an error called "legalism." So, it should be clear that when I am talking about being a slave of Christ, I am not talking about being a slave to any organization, its leaders, or its rules, but only to Jesus and his word. Denominational (or organizational) structures are helpful only insofar as they focus us on Jesus and his teachings in the Bible. Of course, some churches do this better than others.

One modern observer of the church in America put it this way: "No one has ever told me that they are against becoming like Jesus or being conformed to the ways of Jesus; it's the ways and thinking of the organized church that they don't want to conform to."[6] In fair warning, therefore, since I am a Lutheran pastor, there will be (and already have been) Lutheran references. But let us remember that the goal of Lutheranism has always been to keep Jesus as head of the church and to let his word be the

---

6. Kimball, *They Like Jesus*, 75.

only rule. That is what the "Reformation" of the church was about and, in that sense, it still continues.

This does not mean that legalism hasn't crept in now and then, but it does mean (and this is the important thing) that when it does, we keep on "reforming." Because of that, Lutheranism brings some very hard-won lessons to help all Christians gain a better understanding of God's call in his word to be slaves of Christ. But it is important to remember that God's word does not need any extra help or pressure from the church to conform us into "the image of Christ." That same observer of the church said, "We should leave the job of transforming people to the Holy Spirit."[7] Certainly; I would only add that the Spirit works through his word. That is one of those hard-won things I was talking about. Bottom line: being a slave of Christ is something all Christians are called to be.

What Is a Slave?

And there is one more misunderstanding—the misunderstanding of slavery itself. In our modern culture, our understanding of slavery has been greatly influenced by both the history of slavery in America and by the fact that our theological thinking has now been greatly impacted by the rise of both skeptical and materialistic philosophies since the Enlightenment. The latter has turned God into an idea, disconnected from daily life, and the former sees all slavery as inherently evil, almost to the point where any authority that tries to control us is seen as evil. These are like thick, dark lenses in a pair of glasses that blind us to understanding the Bible's teaching about slavery to Christ. Those lenses must come off before we can see clearly. We must get rid of the idea that slavery is about race and racism. Hopefully Part 1 will deal with some of those issues.

In the thought world of the Bible, all human beings are considered slaves, either of sin or of God. In the first chapter of Part 2 on belonging, we shall find that people are dependent creatures, and that means our belief in independence is an illusion. If the heart does not cling to God, it will cling to some worthless or evil thing; it cannot be helped. Dependent beings must have a god. Therefore, slavery to other humans, as we shall see, is understood by Scripture as an evil, even idolatry, but slavery to God is understood as a great good. In Part 3 on serving, we shall find what it is like to get rid of dealing with God as only an idea. Instead, the Bible presents

7. Kimball, *They Like Jesus*, 107.

him as a personal being involved in the world—involved in our personal world. All that we do is in relationship to him. He is our living master, and all we do is in service of him.

There has also been some debate over the definition of slavery itself. And this is important when comparing the way slavery exists in the world with the way it exists with God. Traditionally the emphasis has been on the slave as property—a slave belongs to someone who can do with them as he wants. It logically follows, then, that we must also consider the slave as worker—a slave does what someone else tells them to do.[8] A slave has no will of their own. In recent times, however, there has also been an emphasis on the "experience" of slavery, i.e., the injustice, violence, domination, and "social death" (loss of identity) that slaves endure.[9] In fact, many would define slavery as a system of abuse.

But when we look at slavery in the Roman Empire, it is possible to find some exceptions to this last idea. Although it was the norm, not all slaves were abused; that depended on the master. In human slavery, there is little hope of avoiding abuse because the master's will must be forced on the slave. But a slave might be blessed with a good master or may even be a willing slave. Abuse may not always be a slave's experience and in that sense would not necessarily be part of its definition. Especially in the case where God is the master, there would be no need for any abuse, "social death," or loss of identity. There may even be the opposite—a strong identity, a family of fellow believers, and a happier life because of it.

The importance of finding out "who you are" has become very important in our culture. Our "identity in Christ" has become an extremely popular catchphrase among Christian writers and preachers. As far as I can tell, it seems to have developed from a popular form of psychological counseling called cognitive behavioral therapy, which had its beginnings in the 1960s. It is based on the very common-sense idea that what you believe about yourself and what you tell yourself will affect how you behave. Christian counselors such as Jay Adams and Lawrence Crabb adapted it as a new form of "biblical counseling" in the 1970s. Its basic idea was then picked up and further adapted into popular preaching and teaching by leaders such as Neil T. Anderson, Rick Warren, and Tim Keller in the 1980s and 1990s.

Adopting a Christian identity—who you are in Christ or your new identity in Christ—can have a powerful and positive effect on your life

---

8. Harris, *Slave of Christ*, 107.
9. Byron, *Recent Research*, 27.

Introduction

emotionally and behaviorally. This, it is claimed, will help you with personal problems, changing sinful behaviors, becoming a more mature Christian, and many other things. Even though the popularity of "discovering your identity in Christ" has made it a bit like the snake oil salesman's cure-all for whatever ails you, there is no denying the practical truth it contains. What you believe about yourself will affect the way you behave.

"Our identity in Christ," however, suffers from being a bit abstract; it is not clear what is meant, especially when applied to so many areas of a Christian's life. Those who talk about your identity in Christ will focus on many positive images, such as "child of God," "a minister," "complete in Christ," "a witness," "a friend of God," "a saint," "salt and light," etc. "Slave of Christ," however, rarely makes the list. I assume that is because it sounds negative. But at least "slave of Christ" does not suffer from the problem of being abstract or vague. It is easily grasped, very concrete, and certainly specific. It gives you a clear identity: you belong completely to God, and you serve him. It gives you a clear purpose and direction: obedience and service.

Being a slave of Christ may seem to be too passive and may not appeal to those who like the "spiritual warrior" image. While it is true that the slave is completely dependent on the master who supplies daily bread, clothing, shelter, and even fights your battles for you, still, no one would doubt that it takes the courage of a warrior to do what God wants and be obedient to the point of death.[10] The martyrs witnessed with their lives. "Passive" does not seem to describe the Christian's struggle and our need for courage.

Understanding themselves as slaves of Christ was helpful for first-century Christians, and it can be helpful for us. When we investigate what being a slave of Christ means, you might be surprised to find that it is the most significant truth about who you are. Even so, it may be difficult for many to see slavery in a positive light. The biggest problem will be that slavery is usually understood in our culture as the opposite of freedom. We love our freedom, though our ideas about it are often quite twisted. So, in the next chapter, we will begin to deal with what real freedom looks like and, with the help of its first-century context, what slavery to Christ might look like. Then you can decide in what way these ideas apply to your relationship with Jesus. Frankly, given the often-upside-down nature of God's kingdom

---

10. Ephesians 6:10–20 on the armor of God appeals to the spiritual warrior, but this warrior is on guard duty. He is to "stand." Slaves could not serve in the Roman army, but they could carry weapons in defense of their master. Ephesians 6 may be this kind of thing. God has his own army (Hebrew *Sabaoth*); 2 Kgs 6:17.

in this world, I think you should be prepared to consider that being a slave of Christ may be a "better freedom" than you imagine.[11]

---

11. Card, *Better Freedom*, 21. Card is quoting Ignatius, a second-century martyr, about obedience to Christ.

PART 1

Some "Issues"

> "Don't the Bible say we must love everybody?"
> "O, the Bible! To be sure it says a great many such things;
> but then, nobody ever thinks of doing them."
>
> —Uncle Tom's Cabin[1]

---

1. Stowe, *Uncle Tom's Cabin*, 310.

CHAPTER 1

The Problem of Obedience

"You are slaves of the one whom you obey." —Romans 6:16

It may be surprising to begin with obedience, but this is where any modern consideration of slavery must begin. We have major problems with the idea of obedience, yet it is central to the definition of a slave. The idea of existing only to serve the will of another is why Aristotle defined a slave as a "living tool."[1] Having no will of your own makes you a tool, a machine, a thing, and hence a thing that can be owned. In Greek and Roman law, a slave is a human being, a living thing, but not a legal "person" with rights. This is, of course, the same fiction our Supreme Court applies to unborn babies. This is why the arguments against slavery and abortion are the same, only with abortion, the mother is the owner of another human being and can do with it as she wants.

The idea of not being able to do what we want is abhorrent to us. It was not abhorrent to Aristotle, who was not encumbered with the Judeo-Christian notion of a soul in the image of God, human dignity, or individual rights. The practical problem of slavery, however, wasn't the philosophical problem of whether someone had a will; the problem was how to make someone's will agree with yours. In human slavery, the will of the other must be broken and forced to obey. In slavery to Christ, the will is won over, is given, entrusted, to Christ—its rightful director, ruler, lord. Both could be said to result in obedience, but it is not the same kind of obedience at all. We have a problem telling them apart, as we shall see, and this

---

1. Aristotle, *Politics* 1.125a, quoted in Andreau and Descat, *Slave in Greece and Rome*, 96.

has also twisted our understanding of freedom. We have joined things that are meant to be separated (freedom and unrestrained selfishness) and we have separated things that are meant to be joined (faith and obedience). Whether Catholic or Protestant, modernism has divorced faith and life.

This has become increasingly obvious since the cultural and sexual revolution in the West after the Second World War, which completely changed our culture's value system. Christians simply floated along with the tide. As already noted, Christians are now under pressure to conform to an evolving value system that is coming more and more into line with ancient pagan ones. And we are giving in. It seems clear that modern Christians have a problem with obedience to God. We are reverting along with the rest to a more pagan culture. In the first century, for example, human life had no intrinsic value—unwanted children were killed or exposed and left to die, suicide was a respectable option, and watching people being killed was a form of entertainment. The value of life—and, in fact, all values—were determined by money, power, and pleasure. The Romans, for example, were very pragmatic about this, using any means—war, politics, or murder—to get what they wanted.[2]

All forms of sexual practice (for men, that is)—extramarital sex, prostitution, child rape, and homosexuality—were not just accepted ways of finding sexual pleasure but were more often expressions of power over others. Marriages were made, broken, and remade based on economic and political advantages. The primary function of marriage in the ancient world had little to do with either love or sex but with "rightful heirs" to family position, power, and property. Marriage was a practical family (or business) matter that did not involve any religious or state supervision. The only concern of government with marriage was with the legal issues of property ownership. The philosophers taught that the good life was found through a practical use of reason, not through religion. All of this is the way our modern world is trending. We are headed "back to the future."

When Christianity entered this culture in the first century, it was shocking and revolutionary. Christians did not kill their children. They even took in children that were exposed and left to die. They cared for the weak, the powerless, and the suffering, and they rejected cruelty. They were known for loving acts of kindness. They were also known for sexual purity, something unknown outside of Judaism. All sexual activity outside of marriage, which was God's ideal for the family, was rejected. Christians

2. Harrill, *Slaves in the New Testament*, 3–6.

intended to marry for life with the purpose to love their spouse and raise a God-honoring family, not for personal gain or advancement. They did not think money and power were the highest values but service to Christ and their neighbor. They did not work in any occupation that "glamorized" sin, such as the theater, the arena, or anything to do with idols. They were good citizens, obeyed the law and paid their taxes, but if the state required them to worship idols, they were willing to die rather than submit.

Some historians have claimed that all this unusual behavior by first-century Christians was nothing more than "legalism," or, as we observed before, rules made by the leaders of the church. They claimed that "faith had degenerated into moralism enforced by fear of judgment."[3] "Fear of judgment" meant the fear of rejection by the organized church, as well as from God, if one did not do what they said. This probably says more about these historians than about the early Christians. To those who live in a world of "cheap grace," all obedience is legalism.

Cheap Grace or Obedience?

The term "cheap grace" comes from the book *The Cost of Discipleship* (1937) by Dietrich Bonhoeffer, who wanted to recapture a true understanding of the radical call to follow Christ. He described coming to faith in terms of a total commitment to Christ that sounds very much like slavery, though he did not use that term. The gospel tells us we were bought at a price and now belong completely to another (1 Cor 6:19–20). We serve him, not to become his, but because we are already his. But Bonhoeffer noted that cheap grace forgives the sin but makes no claim on the sinner.[4] "When we are called to follow Christ, we are summoned to an exclusive attachment to his person. The grace of his call bursts all the bonds of legalism. . . . Rather it is the exact opposite of all legality. It is nothing else than bondage to Jesus Christ alone, completely breaking through every programme, every ideal, every set of laws."[5] In fact, he famously adds, "When Christ calls a man, he bids him come and die . . . because only the man who is dead to his own will can follow Christ."[6] This may sound extreme, but this is exactly what a first-century Christian would understand by the title "slave of Christ."

---

3. Green, *Evangelism in the Early Church*, 185.
4. Bonhoeffer, *Cost of Discipleship*, 35.
5. Bonhoeffer, *Cost of Discipleship*, 49.
6. Bonhoeffer, *Cost of Discipleship*, 79.

Part 1: Some "Issues"

Slaves are in "bondage" to another person, an "exclusive attachment" to that person. The owner may command his slaves to do whatever he wants and do with them as he wants. If a free man was sold into slavery in the Greco-Roman world, he became legally dead. His marriage was ended; his children were no longer his; he could own nothing; he even lost his name and was given a new one by his master.[7] He ceased to be a "person" under the law.

"Losing your life," everything the world calls life, was the way Jesus described what it meant to follow him: "Whoever finds his life will lose it, and whoever loses his life for my sake will find it" (Matt 10:39). Jesus is not just talking about martyrdom. Paul explains this call as a complete break with the world: "Set your minds on things that are above, not on things that are on earth. For you have died, and your life is hidden with Christ in God" (Col 3:2–3; see also 5–11). Bonhoeffer comments: "They [followers of Christ] have only him [Jesus], and with him they have nothing, literally nothing in the world, but everything with and through God."[8]

Jesus warns those who would follow him what it means to be dead to the world: "If anyone comes to me and does not hate his own father and mother and wife and children and brothers and sisters, yes, and even his own life, he cannot be my disciple" (Luke 14:26). But having surrendered everything to Jesus, we discover all that we have "with and through God." "Peter began to say to him, 'See, we have left everything and followed you.' Jesus said, 'Truly, I say to you, there is no one who has left house or brothers or sisters or mother or father or children or lands, for my sake and for the gospel, who will not receive a hundredfold now in this time, houses and brothers and sisters and mothers and children and lands, with persecutions, and in the age to come eternal life" (Mark 10:28–30).

Our idea of happiness, however, is directly related to acquiring as many things as we can for ourselves and using them for our pleasure and entertainment (the advertiser's definition of happiness). We believe that the more things we have, the more comforts, the more pleasures we can afford, the more security, the more success, then the more happiness we will have. Solomon had all this, plus the absolute power of a king and the wealth of the world, and discovered that it didn't work. This kind of happiness can never last more than a moment (Eccl 2:10–11). He concluded that trusting God gave him something more important. It gave him contentment

---

7. Andreau and Descat, *Slave in Greece and Rome*, 11.
8. Bonhoeffer, *Cost of Discipleship*, 95.

(Eccl 12:3; Matt 6:33). Jay Carty has insightfully explained what contentment is: "Contentment is a by-product of giving everything you have, are, and ever will be to God and then allowing him to give back everything, except that which will enslave us, and then trusting his decision."[9] Contentment, in other words, comes from knowing that you and everything you have belongs to God, as we shall see again in a later section. Without this, there is very little hope of any lasting happiness.

But cheap grace has had a profound effect on modern Christianity, proclaiming to us a god who is "nice" to all "nice" people, who wants us to have "nice" things and a "nice," happy life. Many Americans who identify on surveys as Christian are really what some researchers are now calling "Moralistic Therapeutic Deists," or MTDs. According to George Barna's research, four out ten American adults now classify in some way as an MTD. Most of these are under fifty years of age, and three-fourths of them still call themselves Christian.[10] An MTD believes in a god who rewards good people with a better life (moralistic), who wants them to be happy and feel good about themselves (therapeutic), and who is not involved in one's life except when needed to fix a problem (deist). The only difference between this and ancient paganism is that it requires a different kind of sacrifice to obtain the favor of the gods. Instead of animals, it requires us to be nice—not good, just "nice."

We sometimes forget that ancient pagan religions had no moral content.[11] You honored and sacrificed to the gods so they would do something nice for you. Obedience was not required. Philosophy was the subject that dealt with virtue and the moral life, and this had nothing to do with the gods. Philosophers each had their own suggestions which you could follow, and these might lead to happiness in life, but this didn't please the gods or gain anything from them. Gaining the gods' favor was done by observing the festivals and sacrifices. Among the educated, philosophy became a sort of practical substitute for the "superstitions" of religion. They felt it was a more reliable way to find happiness than religion. In a similar way, obedience to the will of God has no place in our modern understanding of religion either. Celebrating the festivals of Christmas and Easter is often considered enough to keep God happy. Then we can try to find happiness by living by various philosophies which have nothing to do with God.

---

9. Carty, *Counterattack*, 184–85.
10. Barna, "American Worldview Inventory," 2–3.
11. Beard, *SPQR*, 102–3.

Part 1: Some "Issues"

Barna's research shows that 95 percent of MTDs do not think that obedience to God is necessary.[12]

In the modern world, observed C. S. Lewis, the highest moral value is "kindness,"[13] what I've described as being nice. He believed kindness is what most people mean by the word "love," though he felt it a poor substitute. This "kindness" trumps every other value such as truth, sexual morality, and obeying the law because, in actual fact, it teaches us to "kindly" overlook them all. This is seen as playing well with others. Therefore, Moral Therapeutic Deism has no real moral content, because God makes no real demands on you. There is only the expectation of "kindness." This, and maybe going to church on a special occasion. These are the "sacrifices" that God requires. In the MTD and pagan mind, all it takes is some small sacrifice to make the gods happy with you.

There have always been only two kinds of sacrifice. In Gen 4, both are seen in the very first sacrifices of Cain and Able. C. F. Keil wrote: "Abel's thanks came from the depth of his heart, whilst Cain merely offered his to keep on good terms with God."[14] Sacrifices were meant to be an expression of the love and faith of the heart (Hos 6:6; Matt 9:13), not an economic transaction with God—not a payment for services like health, wealth, or protection for the "privilege" of simply being left alone. God needs nothing from us (Ps 50:7–15; Acts 17:24). Sacrifices are meant to be a response to a God who first loved us, a "listening" to his will and "heeding" it, that comes from faith. The Bible says: "For you [God] will not delight in sacrifice, or I would give it; you will not be pleased with a burnt offering. The sacrifices of God are a broken spirit; a broken and contrite heart, O God, you will not despise" (Ps 51:16–17).

Samuel had to remind Saul: "To obey is better than sacrifice, and to listen than the fat of rams" (1 Sam 15:22). Obedience was to come from the heart. Obedience is not just making your body do what the law requires. F. E. Mayer has put it well: "The attitude of the heart determines the character of a work.... The Christian as a total person is active in good works, and his one standard is love toward God and toward the fellow man. Thus, the Christian's good works are called 'fruits of the Spirit,' while the unbelievers are 'works of the law.'"[15] As we shall see in coming sections, everything

---

12. Barna, "American Worldview Inventory," 2.
13. Lewis, *Problem of Pain*, 40.
14. Keil and Delitzsch, *Commentary*, 1:111.
15. Mayer, *Religious Bodies*, 173–74.

depends on who you serve and why, for even the "righteousness of the Christian is very imperfect and pleases God only for Christ's sake."[16] Faith produces good works like "every healthy tree bears good fruit" (Matt 7:17).

We live in a confusing and immoral world, just as first-century Christians did. Early Christians rejoiced that they belonged to the right master, who had freed them from their old master of sin and death, and so they gratefully served him. Understanding themselves as slaves of a new and better master gave them a clear purpose. "For the grace of God that brings salvation has appeared to all men. It teaches us to say 'No' to ungodliness and worldly passions, and to live self-controlled, upright and godly lives in this present age, while we wait for the blessed hope—the appearing of the glory of our great God and Savior, Jesus Christ, who gave himself for us to redeem us from all wickedness and to purify for himself a people that are his very own, eager to do what is good" (Titus 2:11–14). Their hope could be seen in their lives, their words, and their actions, and it was this living hope that drew countless others to this faith.[17]

In the New Testament, being a slave of Christ was the way to talk about "costly grace." It wasn't that they were trying to be different, as in legalism, to earn happiness or impress God and buy his favor. They were trusting Jesus and following him—not trying to keep a list of rules but rather trying to be faithful to him. In the words of Henry David Thoreau, they were "marching to the beat of a different drummer" (or in Jesus's words in John 10, "listening to the voice of a different shepherd"), and they were willing to go where he led, no matter how difficult or how strange it made them look to others. There are always many competing voices claiming to speak the truth and calling us to follow. But there are, when it comes right down to it, only two "drummers." "Do you not know that . . . you are slaves of the one you obey—whether you are slaves to sin, which leads to death, or to obedience, which leads to righteousness?" (Rom 6:16). There is no third alternative.

Cheap grace tries to create a third way and calls it "freedom." With cheap grace, all is forgiven from the start. It begins with forgiveness and not with belonging to Christ. We are our own masters. Since sin no longer matters, we are free to live any way we want. We need not be obedient to anyone or anything. This is the "good news" (gospel) to a culture which hates and rebels against any form of authority, especially any which may

16. Mayer, *Religious Bodies*, 175.
17. Green, *Evangelism in the Early Church*, 183–88.

deny our desires. Freedom is the right to live in complete selfishness. From this worldview, any kind of obedience is "legalism." Cheap grace says we are free of all masters, while real grace says we are free of all masters but one.

Since there are only the two masters, thinking you are free of all masters will mean that you are in reality obeying the worst master. When you believe you are doing what you want, and it is not what God wants, then you are actually doing what sin and Satan want. If you are not obeying God, then you are obeying this other master. Michael Card, capturing the thought of Paul in Rom 6, observed that the choice is never between slavery and freedom, but "the choice has always only been whose slave you will be."[18]

Real Freedom

The slave of Christ, being free of all other masters, is really free—free of sin and evil and all that causes pain, suffering, death, and separation from God. The slave of Christ is free to ignore all other opinions, free to reject and discard them, if they conflict with the perfect will of Jesus. The will of Jesus is always what is best and right for us, certainly our best hope of happiness now and forever (even if we do not always see it that way). This makes us the freest people on earth, free to be what we were meant to be. This is Christ's definition of freedom: "If you abide in my word, you are truly my disciples" (John 8:31). We are free *from* lies and falsehood and free *to* know the truth and live according to it. "Christian liberty consists in this," writes Francis Pieper, "that Christians are freed from their own will and are now servants of God (Rom 6:22). Likewise, doctrinal liberty consists in this, that Christian teachers are freed from human opinions and bound only by the Word of God."[19] Real freedom comes only with slavery to Christ.

Because this world is so broken and its values so skewed, this kind of obedience appears to be one of the many seeming paradoxes of Scripture: to be rich you must become poor, to be mature you must become childlike, to be wise you must embrace the foolishness of the gospel, to live you must die, and to be free you must be a slave of Christ.[20] But as with most paradoxes, this is only an apparent contradiction. Obedient freedom seems strange to us, but there is nothing illogical about it. The one does not cancel

---

18. Card, *Better Freedom*, 23.
19. Pieper, *Christian Dogmatics*, 1:134.
20. Card, *Better Freedom*, 24.

out the other; they can and do coexist. Luther, for example, in his book *The Freedom of the Christian*, which we will discuss more in the next chapter, shows how we can be both free and a slave at the same time. And there are other ways to view the connection between obedience and freedom as well.

Theologically, there are some Christians who might describe it as the "third" use of the law. In this understanding, "law" means everything in the revealed will of God that tells us what God created us to be and do, our reflection of God's righteousness (*imago Dei*). The first use of this law, or non-religious use, is to remind people what moral, just, and "civilized" behavior looks like, to help create stable and peaceful societies (respect authority, don't murder, steal, lie, etc.). The second use of the law is to show us how far we have fallen "short of the glory of God" (Rom 3:23), or how far our actual behavior falls short of what we are supposed to be. "Through the law comes knowledge of sin" (Rom 3:20). Here the law shows us that, if we are to be right with God, we need a Savior, and it drives us to the cross of Jesus to find forgiveness. It does this throughout our lives because even Christians, who still have a sinful nature, will need continual repentance. But Christians also have a new nature that fights against the sinful one (Rom 7), working toward becoming what God created us to be (1 Thess 4:1–8). We want to please God, but because we have a damaged conscience along with that sinful nature, the new nature requires the guidance and help of God's revealed will to know what pleases God. We do not please God to earn forgiveness, which is already ours in Christ, but to become what after the resurrection we will always be. This is the "third" use of the law. In the confusion of our desires and the many voices telling us what to do, we listen to only one voice, the voice of the one who purchased us with his blood. The slave listens to the voice of his master and follows.

Others might explain the connection of obedience and freedom more psychologically or experientially. For example, some make the comparison that people are "addicted" to sin the way an alcoholic is addicted to alcohol. If you grant such a comparison, then it is interesting to note how Alcoholics Anonymous (AA), in their *Big Book* by Bill W., explains this seeming contradiction between slavery and freedom:

> The alcoholic is an extreme example of self-will run riot, though he usually doesn't think so. Above everything, we alcoholics must be rid of this selfishness. We must, or it kills us! God makes that possible. And there often seems no way of entirely getting rid of self without Him. Many of us had moral and philosophical

> convictions galore, but we could not live up to them even though we would have liked to. Neither could we reduce our self-centeredness much by wishing or trying on our own power. We have to have God's help. This is the how and why of it. First of all, we had to quit playing God. It didn't work. Next, we decided that hereafter in this drama of life, God was going to be our Director. He is the Principal, we are His agent. He is the Father, and we are His children. Most good ideas are simple, and this concept was the keystone of the new and triumphant arch through which we passed to freedom.[21]

The Big Book, like the other "big book," the Bible, understands freedom as replacing one master with another. But the writer also observes that this cannot be done without "getting rid of the self," and that can only happen when "self" is replaced with God.

Being a slave of Christ not only frees us from slavery to sin, death, and the devil, but it also frees us from slavery to the self, especially slavery to our own feelings and passions and the latest trendy philosophies. In Christ, I am no longer a slave to what Sande calls "the world's postmodern standard, which is 'What feels good, sounds true, and seems beneficial *to me*.'"[22] When Paul says, "For freedom Christ has set us free; stand firm therefore, and do not submit again to a yoke of slavery" (Gal 5:1), he is telling us not to go back to these masters which everyone else follows. Pieper defined freedom as being freed from my own will and from other's opinions and depending only on the word of God.

This is the logical outcome of Luther's concept of *sola scriptura* (Scripture alone as the only source of truth). It overrules my own sense of what is true. I may not feel like much of a sinner, but if the Bible says I am one, that is what I am. I may feel like a worthless person that God could never forgive, but if the Bible says I am a forgiven child of God, that is what I am. If something looks right to me, but the Bible says it's not, it's not. If something looks wrong to me, but the Bible says it's not, it's not. This does not mean I don't have to think, that Christianity is mindless obedience. Understanding what I'm seeing and experiencing, then understanding from Scripture what God's will is in that situation, and then figuring out how best to respond, requires the best and clearest thinking I am capable of.

Knowledge may be what you know, but wisdom is knowing what to do with what you know. Understanding God's word requires both. Solomon

---

21. W., *Big Book*, 63.
22. Sande, *Peacemaker*, 14. Emphasis original.

asked God in 1 Kgs 3:9 for wisdom (modern translations often call it "discretion" or an "understanding mind") but what Solomon literally asks for in the Hebrew of that text is a "listening heart" (*levav*). He asks for a mind and heart guided by the mind and heart of God. This is both freeing and demanding. I may no longer need to struggle with "what is truth" (so long as I am looking to Scripture for it), but it is hard work to deal with the twisted nature of our minds and our world in determining what to do with the truth. That requires a "listening heart," a completely humble attitude toward God and his word, and a mind using all of its powers to do it well. The promise is always true: "If you abide in my word . . . you will know the truth, and the truth will set you free" (John 8:31–32).

Certainly, there is nothing more mindless than going with your gut or following a deaf heart. "If it feels right, it must be right and I should do it" and its corollary "If I don't feel like doing it, I shouldn't have to do it" (even if a parent tells me to, a teacher assigns it, or God commands it) can lead to disaster. "Doing what feels right to me" is, in fact, very close to the ancient Greek concept of *hybris*. The Greek playwrights often observed that doing what felt right led to tragedy—an adulterous affair will lead to the Trojan war, "road rage" will lead Oedipus to kill his father, and blind ambition will lead him to unknowingly marry his mother so he can gain the throne. The Greek ideal was to be ruled by the mind, not the passions. The classic Greek virtues were *sophia* (wisdom), *sophrosyne* (good sense and self-control), *dikiosyne* (good judgment, fairness, righteousness), and *epieikea* (reasonableness). They believed in the pursuit of "excellence" in art, math, philosophy, athletics, etc. They looked down on the Romans for pursuing simply "excelling" in power, control, technology, and wealth. Those who wish to pursue great things, however, often come to the same conclusion as the founders of AA and St. Paul: "For I have the desire to do what is right, but not the ability to carry it out" (Rom 7:18).

The New Testament prized these same virtues but understood them as coming only as gifts from a right relationship with God. "The fear of the Lord is the beginning of wisdom" (Prov 9:10). Righteousness is defined by God's commandments (or by his gift of forgiveness). Excellence is doing what God would think is true, honorable, just, pure, lovely, and commendable (Phil 4:8). Paul says, "I strike a blow to my body and make it my slave" (1 Cor 9:24–27), that is, he practices self-control (see v. 25), so that he does not do what his sinful nature wants but what God wants. Or, put another way, his love for God and his desire to please God empowers his will to ignore his sinful feelings so that he can be obedient to God. Even self-control is a fruit of the Spirit (Gal 5:23). Why would anyone do that? Does he do it to earn "points" with God, to earn his favor, or does he do it to "honor God with his body" (1 Cor 6:20)? Was it legalism or a living faith?

Since all we know by nature is the law, legalism is always a danger for human beings. Since our fall into sin, law is our "default" or "factory setting" way to handle every problem or to control our passions. But not all obedience is legalism. Obedience is also found where there is love, a real desire to please God and not appease him. Obedience is also the result of a living faith. There were many witnesses, both Christian and pagan, to the fact that the love of these first Christians was heartfelt and genuine, and that they had a joyous enthusiasm that was often expressed in the things they did and didn't do. They even expressed joy when being killed for their faith.[23]

They were hopeful people in a hopeless world because they trusted in God's grace in Christ instead of in their own goodness. These early Christians weren't just following rules—they were following Jesus, wanting to serve and please him. Their assurance and confidence did not come from the law or from fear of punishment (1 John 4:18). It came only from the gospel, the joy of those who know their guilt has been pardoned and they are right with God. Their confidence was the result of trusting Jesus and his promises. They were living in the freedom of those who serve the right master.

I Am Not a Robot

Let's be clear. I am not talking about Christians making better choices or deciding to live a more committed or dedicated Christian life nor am I simply advocating for a more moral lifestyle. That might very well be legalism. I am not advocating acting like a Christian but *being* a Christian—a different creature. Believe that Christ by his grace claimed you with his cross and rescued you from death and hell, that you belong to him now and always will. As his possession, it is your "duty and delight" to serve him. A slave cannot make better choices, because he makes no choices; he only obeys. A slave cannot commit, because he has already been committed to or captured by another. He cannot follow a lifestyle because he is not conforming to some cookie-cutter pattern or stereotype of what a Christian is to look

---

23. Maier, *Eusebius' The Church History*, 171–78.

or act like. He is unique and his service is unique. Slaves can only live with what God has given, with the talents and gifts we are given. We must live where he has put us, with the situations we must face, truly free to be in that place the person God made us to be.

When filling out forms on the Internet, you may have been asked to check a box that says "I am not a robot." Most people think that is a silly way to find out whether you are a real person and not a scammer's computer program. Why couldn't the scammer simply have his program check such a box? Actually, the form doesn't care about the answer. If you check the box, you are giving permission for the website to check the way the form has been filled in. Programs fill in forms instantly, automatically. People move cursors and type on keypads. In less than a second, it can tell which was used. What the box appears to ask is not the point. It only matters how you got there, whether your answers were machine generated or people generated.

Anyone can fill in all the right answers and tick the box marked "Christian," but what matters is how you got there. Why did you make those choices? Who are you serving? Who is your master, the scammer or the Lord Jesus? Legalism tries to produce all the right behaviors, all the right words, all the right actions, but it's only a dead machine trying to pass a test. There is no life, no right relationship with God through faith in Jesus, no living person freed from death and living under the lordship of Christ. "The love of Christ controls us, because we have concluded this: that one has died for all, therefore all have died; and he died for all, that those who live might no longer live for themselves but for him who for their sake died and was raised" (2 Cor 5:14–15). "The love of Christ" in this verse means both his love for us and our response of love for him. These are always together in a living faith.

The word used for "control" in that verse is *sunecho*, which is also translated as "compels us" or "constrains us." The Greek means "totally claimed by, dominated by, governed by," or, my favorite, "in the grip of." In Greek literature, it is sometimes used of sickness, "in the grip of a fever." Sickness compels us to stop what we are doing and take care of ourselves. The love of Christ compels us to stop what we are doing (taking care of ourselves) and doing what honors Jesus (e.g. taking care of others). We have been infected with gratitude and love for Christ and we can't help ourselves. We want only what Jesus wants (Gal 2:20), and we will fight with ourselves to do it, if necessary. As a slave, a Christian "must" (Luke 2:49; John 9:4) do the will of God, but we are not robots, not machines. Machines do not love. People do, and they act on it.

Another Way?

Rod Dreher, in his popular book *The Benedict Option*, offers a different way for modern Christians to meet the challenges of what he calls this new "dark age."[24] But he looks to the wrong century and the wrong model for help—fifth-century monasticism. Despite the title of his book, he is not advocating that we join a monastery with its call to celibacy, poverty, and obedience, but rather that we adopt its model of retreating from the world and forming separate communities.[25] He calls on Christians to give up trying to change the world with politics (except to protect religious freedom). In his view, all modern institutions are too far gone for Christians to influence them anymore.[26] We are to prepare, instead, to enter a new "dark age" the way the church entered the last dark age.

The best way to survive, he suggests, is to band together in Christian communities, as the Christians did with monasteries, and create "parallel" institutions of our own—our own social support systems, our own schools, etc.[27] This might appeal to many modern Christians who are already withdrawing from the culture and who socialize only with other Christians. I have met Christians who will honestly tell me that they don't have any friends who are non-Christians. Dreher is offering us an even higher wall of separation between being "in the world" but not "of the world." He sees the self-sustaining separate community as a pattern for us to follow.

But the model of monasticism was created for a different time and a different purpose. It developed after the Roman Empire had adopted Christianity, when it was no longer a minority religion in a hostile culture but rather Rome's official religion. It was a time when the persecution of the church in the Empire had ended. There were no new martyrs, no new heroes to look up to in the church. On top of that, half-converted pagans were entering the church in large numbers, lowering the standards of what

---

24. Dreher, *Benedict Option*, 47.
25. Dreher, *Benedict Option*, 48–53.
26. Dreher, *Benedict Option*, 84–87.
27. Dreher, *Benedict Option*, 93. He is certainly right about the need for Christian schools as an alternative to public education, not as a retreat but as a tool to meet the culture.

it meant to be Christian. They were secularizing the church. The monastic movement was a protest against what was happening in the church, and it would also give the church a new kind of hero. It was not a survival tactic. As J. G. Davies says, "The desert fathers indeed fled not so much from the world as from the world in the church."[28] Now, as then, there is no doubt too much "world in the church" today. But that will not be solved by a retreat from the world now any more than it was then.

The first monastic communities, like those started by Basil, had community outreach and service as a goal, but by the time of Benedict this had ceased and they had become turned in on themselves, an end in themselves. If you could no longer sacrifice your body in martyrdom, you could sacrifice it in complete self-denial. The goal was to defeat secularism in the church by creating an elite Christian class that practiced great self-denial, as opposed to the "ordinary" Christians who were only expected to "pray, pay, and obey." Yes, monasteries protected and preserved ancient learning, but at a terrible cost. It turned Christianity into a religion of merit earned with man-made rules of self-sacrifice. This, as it turns out, might be a case when the church did allow faith to degenerate into legalism. It wasn't done by Christians in the first century, however, but by those in the fourth and fifth.

This movement defeated its own purpose because it ended up making the church more secular than it was since most Christians were not expected to lead very "holy" lives. On this Bonhoeffer comments, "The disciples of Jesus must not fondly imagine that they can simply run away from the world and huddle together in a little band."[29] He says, "Let him [the disciple of Jesus] remain in the world to engage in a frontal assault on it and let him live the life of his secular calling in order to show himself as a stranger in this world all the more."[30]

First-century Christians adopted exactly this method. They did not run away from the world but engaged in a frontal assault. As slaves of Christ, they lived very different lives while living very normal lives in the world, showing the love of Christ and serving him by serving their neighbor in their worldly vocations (1 Pet 2:11–19; 3:13–16). Certainly, Christians as members of the body of Christ must exist in communities or congregations for mutual support, encouragement, and for the Christian education of the

---

28. Davies, *Early Christian Church*, 185.
29. Bonhoeffer, *Cost of Discipleship*, 171.
30. Bonhoeffer, *Cost of Discipleship*, 23.

young.³¹ These are not meant to be fortresses but rescue stations for reaching the lost.

To form congregations, we must first form Christians. There is a reason Dietrich Bonhoeffer published *The Cost of Discipleship* in 1937 and *Life Together* in 1938. Discipleship must always precede life together. In *Life Together*, Bonhoeffer said, "We belong to one another only through and in Jesus Christ."³² Community is not something we build and organize (e.g., with a monastic "rule") but a reality discovered and lived out by those completely committed to following Christ—in the real world. Bonhoeffer said, "Christ lived in the midst of his enemies . . . so the Christian, too, belongs not in the seclusion of a cloistered life but in the thick of foes."³³

We sorely need this understanding of faith lived out in the world to meet the challenges of our day, as it helped the first-century Christians meet the challenges of theirs. Only then, knowing who and what we are in Christ, can we stand firm against the increasing attacks of the world, build real community in the world with our fellow believers, and win over those who oppose us. D. S. Russell observed that when the Jews lost their homeland in the early second century, they chose a kind of "Benedict option" with disastrous results. "Unlike Christianity which went out into the Hellenistic world to 'out-think and out-live and out-die' the pagans, it [Judaism] chose for itself the path of separation."³⁴ They withdrew into little communities called "ghettos." Yes, they survived, but they have had to endure constant attempts to annihilate them, even today.

The most telling objection to a retreat from the world, however, is that it is selfish and uncaring toward the lost. It is quite literally letting the world go to hell. It is disobedience to the great commission. We must remember, however, that changing the world must be done God's way. It is just as selfish and uncaring to simply attack those who disagree with us, to bully, destroy, or force others into compliance with our views. Because the world does this (especially in modern politics), it thinks everybody does this, even Christians, and, of course, there will always be some Christians who oblige by "fighting fire with fire," as they might say. But there is a better way as we shall see in chapter 3.

---

31. Dreher, *Benedict Option*, 143–73.
32. Bonhoeffer, *Life Together*, 21.
33. Bonhoeffer, *Life Together*, 17.
34. Russell, *Between the Testaments*, 39.

The Problem of Obedience

I think Dreher is probably correct to observe that our modern secularized Christianity cannot survive the attacks of our modern world. Consider all those who think MTD is Christianity. Church membership is declining rapidly in the Western world. Those who claim to be Christian have become too much like the world around us to resist it. But the answer is not for the "real" Christians to withdraw from the world to protect and defend our way of life. The times call for Christians to understand once more the radical call of the gospel upon their lives, the way of bondage and obedience to Jesus—the way of Bonhoeffer, not Benedict. We must discover again the joy of being the "slaves of Christ."

CHAPTER 2

Isn't "Slave" Just a Metaphor?

"Live as people who are free, not using your freedom as a cover-up for evil, but living as servants [*douloi*, slaves] of God." —1 PETER 2:16

MOST PEOPLE CONSIDER THE phrase "a slave of Christ" to be a metaphor. A metaphor is a comparison of one thing in terms of another. It aids understanding by comparing characteristics of something well known (in this case, slaves) with characteristics of something less well known (being a follower of Jesus). If a metaphor, "slavery" would describe some similarities with being a slave, but not all; it would not be a definition. Remember the definitions we considered for slavery. They include the ideas of belonging to another (property), service (obedience), and social identity (or lack of it). But which of these is this metaphor of slavery referring to, and in what way?

Remember that for many, belonging to God means only that God will take care of us and help us through difficulties. Service to God (obedience) means only that we should be kind to others as much as possible. For them, our "identity" as Christians does not involve changing anything. We have simply added God to our assets so we can keep on living the way we want as if nothing else has changed. In this way, we can still claim that we are "slaves of Christ." That's as far as an MTD Christian, whose confidence is in "cheap grace," will want to take this metaphor.

C. S. Lewis explains: "Some people, when they say that a thing is meant 'metaphorically,' conclude from this that it is hardly meant at all. They rightly think that Christ spoke metaphorically when he told us to carry the cross: they wrongly conclude that carrying the cross means nothing more

Isn't "Slave" Just a Metaphor?

than leading a respectable life and subscribing moderately to charities."[1] Now are these conclusions due just to human ignorance and blindness, or are they problems inherent in the concept of metaphor? Might "slave of Christ" be more than metaphor?

At first it seems that we must take the idea of slavery as a metaphor because it is difficult to see it as literal. For one thing, it appears to be in conflict with the Bible's other descriptions of the Christian life.[2] In John 8, Jesus says, "The slave does not remain in the house forever; the son remains forever. So if the Son sets you free, you will be free indeed" (John 8:35–36). To our modern eye, slave and free appear to be opposites, mutually exclusive, but in the ancient world this would not have been true. When slaves were freed, they did not become independent. They were considered in some sense to be a part of the family which freed them and still had a debt of service (*obsequium*) to their former masters.[3] No one in the ancient world was independent, or "free," in our sense of the word, as we shall see in a later section.[4] A free man, though legally free, could still live as an actual slave to his former master. Jesus does not rule out slave-like obedience in this new relationship with the Son.

Jesus said to his disciples, "No longer do I call you servants [*doulous*, slaves] . . . but I have called you friends" (John 15:14–15). But "friend" and "slave" were not necessarily mutually exclusive categories either. There are many examples from the ancient world where real friendship and love developed between a master and slave. Even in Exod 21, when a Hebrew slave is to be freed, he may elect to stay a slave, saying, "I love my master, my wife, and my children; I will not go out free" (v. 5). Although "no longer call you a slave" sounds like no longer one thing but now another, these categories can overlap.

It would also be hard to think of a Christian as a literal slave of God because of the force and brutality against slaves, which does not fit with the Christian's experience of God. Slaves became slaves by being captured and sold, forced to be slaves against their will. The brutality of slavery is why a slave would never choose to be a slave. Since God doesn't use force with us, we reason that it must not be like real slavery but rather some kind of "servant"— a willing, independent contractor, who will be rewarded for his

---

1. Lewis, *Miracles*, 78–79.
2. Harris, *Slave of Christ*, 149–56.
3. de Wet, *Preaching Bondage*, 21–23.
4. Crook, *Law and Life of Rome*, 55.

work. But what if willingness is neither forced nor a choice, but rather a gift of grace? Faith may not fit the category of either forced or willing, as we shall see in the section on baptism.

The issue of force brings us also to the idea of abuse. Many people think that abuse is the definition of a slave. Since slaves serve against their will, they are physically punished when they disobey, sometimes brutally. Hebrews 12, for example, says God does not punish us like a slave but "disciplines us like a son." The right to discipline or punish any member of the family, child or slave, belonged to the master or father (*pater familia* meant both). In that sense, there was also little difference in the power and position of a child and a slave. The treatment of both depended only on the master's will and purpose. And what if his will and purpose is the same for both? We assume a slave would be abused and a child would not. Both might be, or more to the point, neither might be. What if we find that God makes no distinction (Acts 10:34), that the purposes of God are always to treat us, whether slave or free, in ways that are for our good, that lead to faith and forgiveness, greater trust and obedience in him (Heb 12)? Then whether we are God's slave or child makes little real difference. Both a slave and a child could be "disciplined like a son."

Finally, we could observe that slaves were not usually "adopted" into a family, nor could they legally receive an "inheritance." These were only for free men, yet Christians are said to be given both (Gal 4:1–7). We do not have a lot of information on how Roman law on these issues may have applied to non-Romans, and we know actual practice did vary depending on who you were and where you were. A slave or even a freed slave could be treated like a child, though not technically adopted, as we just noted. Legally, the master could still give gifts as he wished, which could be understood as an inheritance, even if legal categories might be sometimes problematic. Certainly, God is not bound by Roman law and can adopt or give inheritance where he wishes. For now, we must note the possibility that what appear to be contradictions to taking slavery literally may not be contradictions at all.

Many of these ways to describe the Christian life can be helpful and sometimes even inspiring, yet we must not miss the obvious problem of reducing slavery to "metaphor." A metaphor is a comparison, not a definition. With the comparison of a Christian to a slave, we might see only certain similarities that help us understand the Christian life, but we might still miss the greater point. A metaphor means that one is not the other. A

Isn't "Slave" Just a Metaphor?

Christian is not really a slave. A Christian has only some similarities to a slave, and, with metaphors, you get to decide how far to take the comparison. Maybe it is "hardly meant at all," as Lewis said.

But what if being a slave of Christ is not meant to be a metaphor but a statement of fact, a definition? What if we really do belong to Jesus, body and soul, and are really meant to obey him completely? I. A. H. Combes, in the first sentence of her book on the metaphor of slavery in the early church, observes, "Metaphors are dangerous things." Then she quotes D. Davidson with approval: "Understanding a metaphor is as much a creative endeavor as making a metaphor, and as little guided by rules."[5] So, to help us understand metaphors and how they work, she proposed a rubric for dealing with comparisons in Scripture describing our relationship with God:

1. A comparison may be intended to be understood literally—a real situation in which the individual is in precisely the same relationship with the deity as he or she would be with the human equivalent.

2. A comparison may be intended to be understood as a metaphor—it expresses details of the relationship between the human and the divine but does not define it. It may be replaced by a different metaphor when the situation demands, e.g., God as a shepherd. He does not herd sheep, nor does he treat people as animals, but he does own, care for, feed, and defend them.

3. A comparison may be intended to be understood as a symbol—a simple image with one point of comparison where other details are obviously to be ignored, e.g., God as eagle (protector of helpless young) or wind (an invisible power).[6]

Interestingly, she says that the Hebrews called themselves slaves of God in sense number one (see Lev 25:55; 2 Chr 12:7–9), or literally slaves, because of their Oriental culture, where people were always under the power of another. Then she says that Christians called themselves slaves of God in sense number two, or metaphor, because in Greek culture, Greeks considered themselves a free people: citizens, not subjects.[7] She says that although Christians "clearly think they are saying something empirically true" when they call themselves slaves of Christ, "they are not. In spite of

---

5. Combes, *Metaphor of Slavery*, 11.
6. Combes, *Metaphor of Slavery*, 19.
7. Combes, *Metaphor of Slavery*, 42–44.

seeming so literal, this is, of course, still a metaphor. It clearly does not describe an empirically obvious relationship in the manner of the enslavement of one human to another."[8] Perhaps she assumes that abuse must be part of any empirical definition of slavery and therefore cannot describe our relationship with God. She does not explain further. Yet this did not prevent her from understanding the Hebrews as literal slaves of God. Coming out of a Hebrew background, however, it seems likely that the early church would understand itself in the same way as Israel, at least at first.

As Christianity moved into the West there is no doubt that slavery to Christ took on this more metaphorical meaning. The historian J. G. Davies writes: "Faith, in the New Testament sense, is primarily the outcome of an encounter with the living Christ which issues in self-committal and trust; it is therefore to be distinguished from belief in certain propositions. This primitive understanding of faith tended to become obscured in the second century as the Church contended with heretical ideas and developed its own norms and standards of doctrine."[9] He did not mean that Christianity became a different faith. Martyrs do not die for propositions, then or now. He meant the church was forced by its enemies to also become a "thinking" church, responding with apologetics and creedal statements. Since the major intellectual tools of the age were Stoic philosophy and allegorical interpretation, it then became much easier in the second and third centuries to see slavery to Christ philosophically, allegorically, and metaphorically.

But the question is whether this was intended by the apostles in their writings and whether they were understood this way by their first-century audience. They were all Jews (except Luke, generally thought to be a gentile, but who may also have been a Jew) from an Oriental culture. Assuming, as I do, that they were the writers of the New Testament, then the New Testament is likely written from a more Hebraic perspective, as is often seen in the way they use the common Greek with Hebraic meanings. The early church was also initially made up largely of Oriental Jews and gentiles attracted to Judaism, called "Godfearers." Wouldn't one expect continuity here within Jewish culture? Early Christians who call themselves "slaves of Christ," as Combes admits, "clearly think they are saying something empirically true," though she assumes it could not be. Still, it seems to me that the "empirical" evidence, the descriptions in the writings and lives of the first Christians, is on the side of their literal understanding of the term.

8. Combes, *Metaphor of Slavery*, 42.
9. Davies, *Early Christian Church*, 93.

Isn't "Slave" Just a Metaphor?

Still, perhaps "empirical" may not be the best way to understand how the first Christians themselves understood this to be literally true. Perhaps "sacramental" might be better. Luther's famous quarrel with metaphor was over its use to describe the sacrament of the Lord's Supper. He remarked that Jesus did not say, "This is *like* my body and blood." He said, "This is." In the same way, Paul did not say in Rom 1 that he was "like" a slave, or in Rom 6 that we were "like" slaves to God, but he wrote, "Paul, a slave," and, "You have been enslaved to God."[10] Calling us slaves is not a comparison, but, as with the Lord's Supper, neither is it a simple transformation of one thing into another. In modern terms we might call it a "real presence," a "sacramental presence," two things sharing the same time and space (1 Cor 10:16). For example, it seems the Hebrew mind had no problem with the incarnation, Jesus is *Immanuel* that is "God with us" (Isa 7:14; 9:6), two things at once, God and man at the same time (John 1:14). The Greek philosophical mind later argues about how the two natures can exist together. To the Hebrew, God is what he is (Exod 3:14).

We can take the sacrament of baptism as another example. In Rom 6, when one becomes a Christian, one's unrighteous nature is not changed into a righteous one. The new nature and our old unrighteous one coexist, creating the inner conflict Paul describes in the following chapter, Rom 7. "For I delight in the law of God, in my inner being, but I see in my members another law waging war against the law of my mind and making me captive to the law of sin that dwells in my members. Wretched man that I am! Who will deliver me from this body of death? Thanks be to God through Jesus Christ our Lord! So then, I myself serve the law of God with my mind, but with my flesh I serve the law of sin" (Rom 7:22–25). We are at the same time sinner and saint, as Luther famously put it. Although our old sinful nature fights for expression, our new nature does not want it to "live."

Here Luther refers to Rom 6: "How can we who died to sin still live in it? Do you not know that all of us who have been baptized into Christ Jesus were baptized into his death? You were buried therefore with him by baptism into death, in order that, just as Christ was raised from the dead by the glory of the Father, we too might walk in newness of life. . . . So you also must consider yourselves dead to sin and alive to God in Christ Jesus" (Rom 6:2–4, 11). Luther explains this as using the new nature created in

---

10. The "humanly speaking" in Rom 6:19 does not mean "metaphorically speaking" but rather "crudely speaking" or being graphically plain, i.e., "let me be blunt." See Lenski, *Romans*, 429–30.

our baptism to daily "drown" the old nature, which is still with us, killing it with contrition and repentance so we can "walk in newness of life."[11]

Luther talks about letting the "new man" live, but Paul, continuing in Rom 6, is much more exact. He describes this "new man" as a "slave of Christ." This is why the new man does what he does, and how he does it.

> Let not sin therefore reign in your mortal body, to make you obey its passions. Do not present your members to sin as instruments for unrighteousness, but present yourselves to God as those who have been brought from death to life, and your members to God as instruments for righteousness [remember Aristotle's slave as a "living tool" or "instrument"]. For sin will have no dominion over you [NIV has "shall not be your master"]. . . . Do you not know that if you present yourselves to anyone as obedient slaves, you are slaves of the one whom you obey, either of sin, which leads to death, or of obedience, which leads to righteousness? But thanks be to God, that you who were once slaves of sin have become obedient from the heart to the standard of teaching to which you were committed, and, having been set free from sin, have become slaves of righteousness (Rom 6:12–18).

The new man that baptism creates, which makes us also both saint and sinner, also makes us a slave of Christ. Being his slave, we are obedient to him, and we turn away from sin with contrition and repentance. This does not mean we will never sin again. Sin will not "reign" in us and will not be our "master," but in the weakness of our sinful nature, we may slip, be deceived, or give into temptation. The difference is that in our weakness, we fail our master; we do not desert him. We seek his forgiveness with contrition and repentance. To sin deliberately, willfully, and to disobey him without repentance is to choose a new master, becoming a slave again of sin, and so lose the old master and the life he gives. "No man can serve two masters" (Matt 6:24). We may be saints and sinners at the same time, but the saint is also a slave of Christ, and it is this truth that Paul appeals to in Rom 6 as our weapon against the sinful nature.

Being more than one thing, having more than one "standing" or "office" at a time, is not at all the same as having a list of metaphors that describe you. These define you. As we will see in a later section, you can have more than one standing or *status*, in the Roman sense, at the same time. You can literally be a father to one person and the son of another while at

---

11. Luther, Luther's Small Catechism, 24.

Isn't "Slave" Just a Metaphor?

the same time being a husband to your wife and a worker to your boss. In the Roman world you can occupy several *status* at the same time. You can be a patron to one man while at the same time the client of another. You could also be a freedman, a *Latin* (having the rights of a native of Italy) or *peregrini* (having the rights of a native of another province), an *incola* (temporary resident) or *coloniae* (Roman citizens living outside Italy) all at once.[12] To Paul you can be a child, a slave, or freeman (Gal 4:1; 1 Cor 7:22) depending on which relationship he is talking about at the time. But they can all coexist.

An Example

Peter tells us in 1 Pet 2:16, "Live as people who are free, not using your freedom as a cover-up for evil, but living as servants [*douloi*, slaves] of God." We may not like the sound of that word "slave," but these words from Peter may have shocked readers in the first century even more since seeing slaves and dealing with them was a part of their daily world, and they knew its darker side better than we do. Because of the negative baggage that comes with the word, even today, New Testament translators often render the word *doulos*, slave, with "servant." After all, to them it is just a metaphor.

Murray Harris, who was on the translation team for the NIV, protested that the word *doulos* should be translated as "slave" not only because it is a more literal translation but because it also conveys a different meaning than *diakonos* or "servant."[13] Chris de Wet says, "The term *doulos*, in Pauline literature, was not a synonym for *diakonos*. . . . The point is that the metaphor does not work if it is reduced to a form of paid servanthood (though slaves could also receive payment and rewards). . . . The potency and radicalism of the metaphor lie in its extremity. The slave is one who has no agency outside of the volition of the master; the will of the slave is renounced and totally subservient to that of the slaveholder. Any authority the slave has is not his own; it is a transplanted and surrogate authority."[14] The same can be said for the Hebrew word *eved*, which means "slave" but is often translated as "servant." Hebrew had another word for servant, *misharath*, from *shara*, "to serve." "Slave" comes out of a whole context of relationships that can only be understood against that context. It has seemed to me that many

---

12. Crook, *Law and Life of Rome*, 37–38.
13. Harris, *Slave of Christ*, 18.
14. de Wet, *Preaching Bondage*, 47.

modern treatments of slavery in the New Testament suffer from, well, being modern.

Our modern ideas about freedom, independence, relationships, belonging, human rights, work, family life, society, and authority are all so different from the first century that they warp our understanding and our grasp of what it meant in the first century to be a slave of Christ. Of course, people are people, and we share ideas, experiences, and emotions across history. But sometimes the differences really do matter.

There are a surprising number of differences in a first-century worldview that will challenge our modern assumptions. Certainly, there are helpful guides, past and present, like Harris and de Wet, who can help us to understand these differences, but I have found that Luther has some advantages they lack.

First of all, he lived in a different age, in the transition between the ancient and the modern age with one foot in each world, so to speak. The worldview of his age was still based on a hierarchy of responsibility and obligation which it inherited from the ancient world. This would soon be replaced by modernism with a materialistic worldview based on competition, survival, and power. C. S. Lewis would describe the old worldview as the "discarded image" because it was left behind and replaced with a materialistic worldview.[15] In the chapter on serving, we will take a closer look at this older system and what we can learn from it, but we should at least note here that, in Luther's worldview, there could be no freedom without responsibility. He also lived in an age of high scholarly interest in the Bible. He was a professor of Old Testament and mastered both Hebrew and Greek, becoming an excellent translator, able to make the world of the Bible come alive for the ordinary person. His translation influenced the first English translations and is still consulted by translators today. So, what would Luther do with a Bible passage like 1 Pet 2:16?

First Peter 2:16 reads: "Live as people who are free, not using your freedom as a cover-up for evil, but living as *slaves* of God." This is confusing to us. How can you live as a free person and slave at the same time? In the modern mind, these can only be opposites, contradictions, either/or. And further, because of our firm belief in individualism and our strong resistance to authority, we would prefer to take "slave" as only a metaphor for a servant. That would allow us to hear only the part about "living in

---

15. Lewis, *Discarded Image*, 216–23.

freedom." Thus, the modern way to approach this conundrum is to talk about metaphors. "Slave" is only a metaphor, but the real thing is to "live free."

The problem of being both free and a slave at the same time might make some sense in the Roman world. As we have seen, Roman concepts of *status, familia,* patronage, freedom, and slavery could, and sometimes did, overlap. For example, if you were under the control of a *pater familia,* you were, as Paul observed, "no different than a slave" (Gal 4:1). Freedmen were often still called "slaves" because they continued to owe loyalty and labor to their former master. If you were *liber homo bona fide serviens* (a free person wrongly enslaved), you could even be legally a slave and free at the same time.[16] It would not have been impossible to overlap the concepts of slave and free, but it would have seemed very odd. In the brutal world of human slavery, no one, being free, would want to remain a slave. But that was because their masters were Romans and not Jesus.

Luther explained how a Christian, though free, may remain a slave. In his book *The Freedom of the Christian,* he began with this famous premise: "A Christian is a perfectly free lord of all, subject to none. A Christian is a perfectly dutiful servant of all, subject to all."[17] In that book, Luther develops what it means to be a part of the "priesthood of all believers." The phrase comes from 1 Peter: "But you are a chosen race, a royal priesthood, a holy nation, a people for his own possession, that you may proclaim the excellencies of him who called you out of darkness into his marvelous light" (1 Pet 2:9). As priests, we are God's representatives to the world and are to serve him by serving others as our spiritual sacrifice. We are free from sin and hell, "lords of all and subject to none," but, once free, we are then obligated to do everything within our power to free others. We are "subject to all," especially to helping them find their freedom in Christ.

Luther is here only echoing Paul in 1 Cor 9:19: "Though I am free and belong to no one, I have made myself a slave to everyone, to win as many as possible." This is why Paul says he does not preach "voluntarily" but "under "compulsion" (1 Cor 9:16–18, my translation) and why he "beats his body and makes it his slave" so "that by all means I might save some" (1 Cor 9:22, my translation). Grace has both set him free and has made him a slave, and that grace is why he is enslaved in the service of Christ for others. This

---

16. Crook, *Law and Life of Rome,* 58.
17. Luther, *Freedom of the Christian,* in Dillenberger, *Martin Luther,* 53.

explains the context of 1 Pet 2:16 without having to turn "slaves of God" into a metaphor.

When the modern mind hears "slave" we think: "Relax, God doesn't mean you are literally a slave. That would be demeaning, insulting, and deprive you of your freedom to make up your own mind—the right to be who you want to be. It only means that, like a good master, he will take care of us (food, clothing, house, car, money, health) and give us directions (not orders), and we, like valued "servants" ("free-agents"—remember the word "free"), are to interpret those directions and carry them out as we think best." Treating "slave of Christ" as metaphor allows us to keep that greatest of all modern virtues: the freedom to do whatever we want, or put another way, the freedom to be disobedient.

Living in the Real World

A person's worldview, the assumptions one makes about the world, impacts the way we use language, especially metaphor. Combes observed that changes in culture and time will change our understanding of a metaphor.[18] This is because all things are understood in terms of our worldview. As C. S. Lewis once said, "I believe in Christianity as I believe that the sun has risen; not only because I see it, but because by it, I see everything else."[19] He meant that Christianity not only helped him make sense of God, it also helped him make sense of everything else in the world. A worldview is a system of ideas about the world, a consistent view of reality. Modern worldviews are very different from Lewis's and those of the first century, but it is through them that people "see everything else." Our brain fits all things into some system of thought or model of reality that helps make sense of our experience, or tries to. Often there are inconsistencies, sometimes large ones, depending on the worldview. Lewis found Christianity to be the best fit for reality and was always ready to defend it as such.

We have already mentioned materialism and the view that everything evolves as one such worldview. It is the magic process that has become the lens through which we now understand everything in our world. By definition, it rules out everything supernatural. Matter and energy are all that exist. The other popular worldview today is sometimes called existentialism. Man is free to act and by his choices creates the reality he experiences. At

18. Combes, *Metaphor of Slavery*, 11.
19. Lewis, *Weight of Glory*, 92.

first this philosophy was about making responsible choices to change the world into what you imagined it could be and living with the consequences, but eventually it moved to choosing a world you imagined to be, creating your own reality by choosing your own truth. This is why we can not only choose how to behave but also things like what sex we want to be, not the sex we are. We choose the kind of God we think should exist, and not the God who does exist. In traditional thinking, we do not choose what is true. I know there are philosophical debates about reality, but the soundest and I think most probable view is that reality (i.e., truth) exists outside of us and that the natural world, or reality, is stamped by the character of the God who made it—though of course it is now fallen. This is the "watershed" point that distinguishes a traditional worldview from the more modern relativistic or constructionist views. I am not going to delve into the finer points of these philosophies; I just want you to know which side of the "continental divide" we are now on.[20]

Coming to faith, then, isn't choosing a god we want to believe in. Coming to faith is like waking up from a dream and discovering the God who is there. We really aren't the person we thought we were, and reality isn't the reality we thought we were living in, and the real God isn't the kind of God we thought he was. The spirit of God working in his word opens our eyes. The word of God is the lens through which we see everything else. Looking through the eyes of faith, we find ourselves looking at the real world, the one where a triune God lives, the one broken by sin. We find that we are broken sinners who have been rescued by the death of his Son on a cross. We find that we belong to him and will live with him forever. We find that we are here to serve him by serving our neighbors and helping them to discover this real world and live in it with us. It is not a world of our making or of our imagining. God enlightens us with his gifts. It's as if his Spirit working through the word turns on a light in a dark room so we can see what we could not see before. Our eyes are opened, a light is turned on, and we see by his light (Ps 36:9).

We find that our thoughts and our imaginings must submit to the revelation of God's word. My reason can understand much of reality, but reason, too, must submit to revelation because my reason cannot know all of reality. I am a creature living within the system and cannot step out of it. I cannot choose God; he reveals himself to me in his word, reveals reality to me, and allows me to see it and to live in it with him. The reality is that we

---

20. See a discussion in Trueman, *Rise and Triumph*; Lewis, *Abolition of Man*.

were slaves to sin and didn't even know it. But God changed all that. He has made us his slaves, slaves of righteousness (Rom 6), to be the holy people he created us to be. We do not have a freedom *to* sin but freedom *from* sin, not only freedom from guilt but the freedom to say "no" to sin.

Perhaps we should stop a moment and point out that any definition of reality is a religion. For example, science has not proven that matter and energy are all that exist or that *if* anything spiritual does exist it is completely irrelevant and unimportant. This is not a conclusion of science; it is an assumption in the philosophy of materialism and of many modern scientists. Such a thing cannot be proven; it is only an assumption about reality, not science. It is a belief, an article of faith, a creed. Science was invented by Christians who assumed that since an intelligent God made the universe and it was the product of an orderly logical "mind," therefore our minds, made in his image, could also logically understand it and discover how God "did it." Science has since been taken over by those with materialist assumptions. Ironically, they continue to use logic and mathematics in their theories even though there is no reason why a materialistic universe should behave logically or mathematically, unless, again, you simply believe that it does. The best explanation for a complex, orderly universe remains an intelligent designer.

Christians invented the scientific method as an important way of logically finding truth about the physical world. But the most reliable source of truth is not always experience, logic, and reason. Our logic can be wrong. If the world is created, the most reliable source of truth must be whatever the creator of the universe reveals about it in his word. There is no conflict between science (as a method) and religion, but there is a conflict between two religions with differing assumptions about reality. There *is* a conflict between the religion of materialism and Christianity. Our courts have not understood that it is impossible not to teach religion in our schools because any time you teach that something is "real" (true) and something else is "not real" (not true), you are teaching religion.

From the worldview we have been describing, neither materialists nor existentialists live in the real world. It is a fantasy world, and everything they see and experience is bent to fit into this kind of world. In the words of Lewis, "By it, they see everything else."[21] Layers in the earth are caused by millions of years, not a flood; the many dinosaur bones that contain carbon-14 (that measures thousands, not millions, of years) must be

---

21. Lewis, *Weight of Glory*, 92.

Isn't "Slave" Just a Metaphor?

"contaminated"; some dinosaur bones have soft tissue that must have somehow survived for millions of years, etc. Christians live in the real world, God's world, and that should change the way we see everything, spiritual and material. There is only one reality, one world, one truth.

Coming to faith is to enter the real world and not just something that happens inside a person, a mental, existential, or a "spiritual" thing. It isn't just the heart that responds to Jesus; the whole person responds to Jesus. Gnosticism, an ancient idea still with us today, divides matter and spirit, body and soul, and then dismisses the physical and the body as unimportant (in Eastern thought, even "unreal"). Materialism does the opposite and dismisses everything but the physical. The Bible deals with us as a body/soul, a physical/spiritual being (Gen 2:7), united to form one person. And we respond to God both physically and spiritually. Bonhoeffer wrote, "When Jesus says 'come' we don't just believe that it is possible. With Peter, we must get down out of the boat and start walking."[22] "Faith apart from works is dead" (Jas 2:26) because otherwise it would not be a real faith for real people in the real world. As the old saying goes, it is faith alone that saves, but faith is never alone.

Bonhoeffer, in commenting on Eph 2:8–10, compares the creation of saving faith to the creation of the world and then our sanctification, or life of good works, to God's preservation of the world.[23] I think that is very suggestive. In a single act God created a functioning world. When he made the stars, they were already shining on earth though light-years away. When he made the world, it was already spinning. When he made the animals, they were already moving. So also, when he creates faith in the heart, it is already acting in good works. As F. E. Mayer says, the distinction between faith and works is a "logical distinction, not a chronological differentiation; a distinction, not a separation; the one an act in the heart by God and the other an act in and by man; the one the complete and present victory over every foe, the other the continuous battle between the Christian and his enemies; the one as the 'already,' the other as the 'not yet.'"[24]

Put another way, you can talk about a machine and the running of the machine as if they were separate. Sometimes you may need to, especially when the machine is broken. But a machine that isn't running is "dead" (Jas 2:17), just a pile of parts. But when it is running and doing what it

---

22. Bonhoeffer, *Cost of Discipleship*, 56–57.
23. Bonhoeffer, *Cost of Discipleship*, 250, 266–68.
24. Mayer, *Religious Bodies of America*, 159.

was designed to do, then it is "alive." God once breathed life into a lump of clay, and still today, through his word, God breathes (2 Tim 3:16) faith into spiritually dead people and makes them alive. "But God . . . even when we were dead in our trespasses, made us alive together with Christ. . . . For by grace you have been saved through faith. And this is not of your own doing; it is the gift of God, not a result of works, so that no one may boast. For we are his workmanship, created in Christ Jesus for good works, which God prepared beforehand, that we should walk in them" (Eph 2:4-10).

Notice the whole person responds in faith: the mind (with a Christian worldview), the heart (with trust and confidence in God—the saving part) and the body (with obedience). Christ redeems the whole person, hence the resurrection of the body and not just a heaven full of souls. Those who believe in "cheap grace" often separate the soul from the life of the body (like the gnostics mentioned above). When they read things like "obedience of faith" among those "called to belong to Jesus Christ" (Rom 1:5-6) they get confused. If you understand that when God gave you faith, he made you a slave of Christ, you will have no problem in understanding this. Being a slave of Christ may be only one of the things we are, but according to Rom 6 and 7, it is to be our primary identity. In Rom 1:1, "Paul, a slave of Christ Jesus" comes even before "an apostle set apart for the gospel of God." Paul is both a slave of Christ and an apostle of Christ at the same time, but slave comes first; it will determine what kind of an apostle he will be. All Christians are slaves of Christ Jesus first, and whatever else they are (father, mother, son, daughter, husband, wife, worker, or apostle) comes second (see 2 Pet 1:1; Jas 1:1; Jude 1).

Would you identify yourself first and foremost as a slave of Christ? Do you think of yourself that way? Well, you may ask, what way is that? What should it mean in our time and place to think of ourselves as slaves of Christ? It will help to understand "slave of Christ" in its New Testament and first-century context so we can better see how this can fit our time and place. As to why one would want to be one, well, that is answered not in understanding slavery but in understanding the master, Christ Jesus.

CHAPTER 3

How Can Slavery Be a Good Thing?

> "Most of all, perhaps, we need intimate knowledge of the past. Not that the past has any magic about it, but because we cannot study the future, and yet we need something to set against the present, to remind us that the basic assumptions have been different in different periods and that much which seems certain to the uneducated is merely temporary fashion."—C. S. Lewis[1]

Is SLAVERY A GOOD thing or a bad thing? The universal answer of history is that it is not a good thing. Slavery has been responsible for a horrible amount of abuse, pain, suffering, and death. What kind of a God would want us to be slaves? Does God approve of one of the greatest evils in the world? Many people are surprised to find that the Bible does not call for the abolition of slavery. It seems to accept it as a normal part of life. The Old Testament has laws concerning the humane treatment of slaves but does not question the existence of slavery. In the New Testament, Paul, in his letters, urges slaves to serve their masters well, and even writes a letter to a slave owner, Philemon, urging him to forgive the runaway slave that Paul is returning to him. Paul certainly does not question the existence of slavery either.

Throughout most of history, people could not imagine a world without slavery. C. S. Lewis warns us when considering a historical issue like slavery, "There is no more tiresome error in the history of thought than to try to sort our ancestors onto this or that side of a distinction which was not

---

1. Lewis, *Weight of Glory*, 28.

Part 1: Some "Issues"

in their minds at all. You are asking a question to which no answer exists."[2] The only moral issue for them was how you treated your slaves, not whether you should have them or not. As we shall see, the Bible, particularly its teaching about the value of human life, would have a major influence on the understanding and practice of slavery in the West. Yet Christianity, as a historical movement, has not always been biblical. The influence of time and place has had its effect on those in the past as it has on us. Christianity, especially after the Reformation, began to have a reforming influence also on social and political thinking, producing many of the great reform movements of the eighteenth and nineteenth centuries.

Today, however, as we noted, the influence of the Bible on our society is declining. Human rights, cut free from a biblical foundation, have become confusing. What would the ancients have thought about the choice of gender as a human right? On the other hand, our modern views on abortion and mercy killing would have made perfect sense to them. We may now see slavery for the evil it is, but then we are still getting other things wrong. We have no place to sit in judgment of the past. In our time we have evils to match or surpass it. "For my thoughts are not your thoughts, neither are your ways my ways, declares the LORD" (Isa 55:8). "The LORD saw that the wickedness of man was great in the earth, and that every intention of the thoughts of his heart was only evil continually" (Gen 6:5). These verses are just as true today as they were then. As Lewis suggests in that quote at the beginning of this chapter, sometimes our best hope of understanding our own time more clearly is by examining the past. That is what this chapter is for.

It is certainly true that early Christians made no attempt to abolish slavery and even continued to own slaves themselves. Although, to be fair, no one else in the ancient world made any attempt to abolish slavery either, not even former slaves. In the West, as the Roman Empire fell, slavery was replaced with other forms of domination that gradually led to increasing degrees of freedom—serfs, peasants, sharecroppers, wage labor. But with the discovery of the new world and the brutal takeover of large tracts of land, slavery to work these lands presented an irresistible economic temptation. Africans were captured and sold as slaves throughout the new world, creating a form of slavery unique to the Americas—a specific ethnic group with dark skin working exclusively on large agricultural plantations. Asians and Latinos were later abused in similar ways.

---

2. Lewis, *Weight of Glory*, 86.

How Can Slavery Be a Good Thing?

This kind of ethnic slavery was unknown in the ancient world. They did not use ethnic markers such as skin color to categorize or stereotype people. The ancient world was much more color blind.[3] Of course, ethnic differences were "seen," but they were mostly ignored as unimportant. Slaves came from every ethnic group, and they could be found in any occupation doing any kind of work, from hard labor, such as working in a mine or being domestic servants, to being doctors, businessmen, and government administrators. Our modern word "slave" does not come from African slavery but from "Slav," meaning the Slavic people of Eastern Europe who the Vikings (Rus) captured in large numbers during the Middle Ages and sold to the Muslim Empire. In Europe at this time, slavery was being transformed into serfs, sharecroppers, and into a class-based economy. It wasn't until Europe began to colonize the rest of the world that slavery was revived to exploit conquered people from different cultures with different skin colors—yellow, red, and black.

Slavery an *Adiaphoron*?

When looking at the question of slavery, the very first thing to understand is that the early church, as Judaism did before it, used a very dangerous and unhelpful way of understanding slavery, which it borrowed from Stoic philosophy. It used the word *adiaphoron* to describe slavery.[4] This word is not found in the Greek of the New Testament, even though St. Paul is supposed to have taught it. In Greek, the word means "indifferent" things. The Stoics said that things like beauty/ugliness, health/illness, poverty/wealth, slave/free, things in which you had no choice, which did not deal with good moral choices (virtue) or bad moral choices (vice), were simply things to be ignored or accepted. They were the "givens" of life to which a stoic was to be indifferent. The important thing to a Stoic was choice, what you did with what you were given.

Often, Stoics would say that a morally good person was free to follow their reason even if a slave, and a morally bad person was a slave to their passions even if free. Unfortunately, this sounds close to what Paul said in 1 Cor 7:22: "For he who was called in the Lord as a bondservant is a freedman of the Lord. Likewise he who was free when called is a bondservant of Christ." But Paul is not talking about people who make morally good

3. Beard, *SPQR*, 86.
4. Ramelli, *Social Justice*, 46–59.

choices as opposed to those who make morally bad choices. He is talking about sinners forgiven in the eyes of God through faith in Jesus and freed from sin to serve God in whatever their outward condition. He is not talking about our moral life; he is talking about the Christian life. And it is helpful to remember the difference.

In the Bible, good and evil are not just about our moral choices but about how closely *all* things align with the will and design of God. "And God saw everything that he had made, and behold, it was very good" (Gen 1:31). Sin describes broken things, things that fall short of perfection, of the way God made them in the beginning (Rom 8:19–23; Matt 5:48; Heb 7:11). Our first parents made a wrong moral choice, but the consequences of that sin were a broken and rebellious heart in all their descendants (Rom 5:12–21) and a broken and rebellious physical world that does not work as it should. For with the curse of sin not only man dies, also all things in nature die, all things fall apart.

What we call the law of entropy says that everything naturally moves toward death and disorder. Paul said, "The creation itself will be liberated from its bondage to decay"—"enslaved" to sin, and it, along with sinful man, is waiting to be restored to its perfect condition on the last day (Rom 8:21 NIV). Many people think that sin is only the bad moral choices we make, but they are wrong. Sin is the brokenness within man and in all creation, and the cause of every evil. Sin is a condition, not an action. Bad moral choices are only the result, the symptoms of a broken humanity. Sin and its cure through forgiveness in the cross must go much deeper into creation to include systems, relationships, nature, and all things out of alignment with God's will. Not just the abusive actions within slavery are sin, but the system itself can be sin.

Ilaria Ramelli is no doubt correct in saying that the Stoic idea of *adiaphora* had a profound effect on early Christianity and its view of slavery. In this view, slavery was something "indifferent" and did not need to be abolished. But she is wrong when she says that St. Paul and the New Testament taught this.[5] The New Testament lives within a different worldview, in which the whole creation is in bondage to sin. Therefore, everything in it is going according to God's will or against it (1 Tim 4:1–4; Phil 4:8). Nothing is indifferent. Everything serves either darkness or light. There are only these two kingdoms (1 Pet 2:9).

---

5. Ramelli, *Social Justice*, 113–14.

The early church was influenced by the world it lived in. It "Christianized" the Stoic concept of *adiaphora* by defining it, not as where no moral choice is possible but where no moral direction is given by the Bible. This was generally understood legalistically as things not covered by a clearly written directive or command. The Germans called these things *mitteldinge* (middle things), things between what is commanded and what is forbidden. Assuming these things were therefore morally "neutral," you were free to use them as you thought best. Thus, the idea of "indifferent" or "makes no difference" clung to the word, creating all kinds of problems. If the Bible didn't specifically forbid something (like slavery), then everyone felt you were free to use it.

In our discussion of "cheap grace," we found that just because we are not saved by being good does not mean that God is "indifferent" about whether we do good or not. In a similar way, just because there is no direct command in the Bible about something does not mean that God is "indifferent" about it. It may be true that not everything is black and white, but that doesn't mean that everything is gray. Very early in the Reformation, the Lutherans discovered that *adiaphora* could be used dishonestly to defend doing things that should not be done, and so they placed limits on its use in Article 10 of the Formula of Concord.[6] They decided that what *adiaphora* depended on was not whether it was something you could get away with but rather whether something was being used to honor God or not.

Even though the Bible does not use the concept of "indifferent" things, it is true that there are things not discussed in the Bible that may be used in more than one way. Even if not a matter of right or wrong, we still cannot be indifferent to better or worse. The Bible is not a book of law for every situation in life. It requires us to apply its principles, to think about the best way to honor God. And so, it gives us a specific principle for handling "middle things" or *adiaphora*. "'All things are lawful,' but not all things are helpful. 'All things are lawful,' but not all things build up. Let no one seek his own good, but the good of his neighbor" (1 Cor 10:23–24). The ESV puts "all things are lawful" in quotation marks because in the context, it is a slogan used by the Corinthians to excuse all kinds of bad behavior not expressly covered by God's law. All such *adiaphora*, things "lawful" or not expressly forbidden according to God's word, must be judged by the standard of whether it is good for us in our relationship with God ("build up" is always used in this way), and especially whether it is good for others.

---

6. Tappert, *Book of Concord*, 610–16.

By this standard, the institution of human slavery is impossible to justify. Worldviews without a concept of good and evil (e.g., materialistic evolution) might try, but thankfully they often fail to convince.

Harris makes an interesting observation by saying that the position of Scripture on slavery is simply that "the state of slavery is irrelevant to your relationship with God."[7] This may be true for the *state* of the slave himself (see 1 Cor 7:21–22; 2 Cor 5:16). Galatians 3:28 says, "There is neither Jew nor Greek, there is neither slave nor free, there is no male and female, for you are all one in Christ Jesus." There are only two categories for humanity left in the New Testament: those in Christ and those not in Christ. But what about the human institution of slavery? Because it does not affect our relationship with God, is it also irrelevant? Is it none of our concern? That question must be answered by "Is it good for us and for our neighbor?," and more broadly, "Does it honor God?" If it fails that test, it most certainly affects our relationship with God because it is then a sin against our neighbor and a sin against God.

This is where the Stoic concept of *adiaphora* becomes dangerous and is used as a smoke screen for evil. Charles Hodge, the head of the theology department at Princeton and perhaps the most famous theologian in America before the Civil War, was called upon to give the church's view on slavery. In the *Princeton Review* of 1836 he wrote, "Both political despotism and domestic slavery belong in morals to the *adiaphora*, to things indifferent. They may be expedient or inexpedient, right, or wrong according to circumstances. Belonging to the same class, they should be treated the same way. Neither is to be denounced as necessarily sinful, and to be abolished immediately under all circumstance and at all hazards."[8]

Notice that Hodge is appealing to the Stoic concept of *adiaphora* as something which is morally neutral and therefore "indifferent," and not the biblical principle found in 1 Cor 10:23–24, things used for the good of the neighbor to honor God. He is using *adiaphora* as a smoke screen to suggest that human slavery can be used without sin. He was understood that way and probably wanted to be understood that way. He does say, to his credit, that the *abuse* of either despotism or slavery is a sin. Like the Stoics, he claims it is not the institution of slavery which is evil but what you do with it. Yet, that is the problem. How can either dictatorship or slavery function without violence and abuse? To this argument, Harriet Beecher Stowe

7. Harris, *Slave of Christ*, 59–60.
8. Cho, "Slavery," para. 6.

How Can Slavery Be a Good Thing?

writes in her famous antislavery novel *Uncle Tom's Cabin*, "Talk of the abuse of slavery! Humbug! The thing itself is the essence of all abuse!"[9]

It is not just a matter of "all power corrupts, and absolute power corrupts absolutely"—Lord Acton's famous saying. The power to enslave a person is not just power over others but a Satanic perversion of the order of creation, in which God alone is master and owner of all. For a man to own another man is for man to put himself in God's place—it is idolatry (Rom 1:18–23). In this sense it is the "essence of all abuse." Stowe may have meant only that abuse is always a part of human slavery and despotism. It is true that no human being can use either the institution of dictatorship or slavery without force, violence, injustice, and cruelty—without sin. The only one who can use either of these institutions without sin is God alone. Not only is he perfectly just in claiming us as his possession, but he does not need to use force. He restores hearts to willing obedience. He is the only true *despotas*, the master of those he created, freed, and rules with love (Deut 10:17; 1 Tim 6:15). Slavery to him is not the evil that human slavery is. An idolator who puts himself in the place of God, on the other hand, must always side with the demons, and may, in fact, become one.

Another problem with the Stoic view is that it asks us to accept things as they are when no choice seems possible. We live in a world where choices are limited: where to live, what to eat, what to wear, what job we have, who we marry, what activities we enjoy, etc. And it is true that many choices are not open to us. We can only eat the food available to us, live in houses we can afford, work in jobs we are hired to do, marry someone who will have us. We can be born into a dysfunctional family, may have to flee our homes in wartime, or we may be forced into slavery. Evil is often outside our control. We may not be able to stop it, but that does not mean it is reasonable to accept it. "Do not be overcome by evil, but overcome evil with good" (Rom 12:21). We must do what we can against evil even when our choices are limited.

The ancients thought that slavery was forced on the slave (by nature, culture, government, history, the gods, etc.) and that there was no other choice. There was no moral choice for the slave except to live morally within it; no moral choice for the master except how to treat his slaves well. It seems that only one church father, Gregory of Nyssa, in the fourth century, asked the obvious question that no one else seemed able to see: The slave may have no choice, but what about the man who owns the slave? Doesn't

---

9. Stowe, *Uncle Tom's Cabin*, 310.

he have the choice not to own slaves? Isn't this also a moral choice? Gregory argued from the creation of man that no one can possess another human being because they already belong to God.[10] He said that slavery was an offense to God and to humankind and ought to be eliminated from society. As Ramelli summarizes, "He was the only church father to condemn slavery de jure and de facto."[11] He called on every Christian slave owner to renounce slavery and free their slaves. Realistically he knew that, even if all the Christians did this, it would probably not change the society which allowed it. Still, he felt Christians, at least, should do it.[12]

Gregory's call to action, however, was dismissed by most because of the times in which he lived. The fourth century was the high point of Christian asceticism. Christian asceticism was a movement that advocated living simply, caring for your own needs, and giving away all the rest of your property (including slaves) to show how faithful you were to God. I particularly like Ramelli's definition of an ascetic as "a specialist in self-denial."[13] In most ages people have never been much interested in self-denial. This was viewed as something only for elite Christians who had a special calling to "give up the world," not something for every Christian. This was the time, as we noted earlier, of the growing monastic movement and the pursuit of Christian perfection through self-denial. Giving up your slaves or other property to serve God was only for the holy few. It was just not practical for the ordinary Christian.

Gregory's biblical reasons to give up your slaves based on creation and injustice were simply heard as an appeal for asceticism. This is just one more example of how we can make obedience optional. "It's not meant for everybody," therefore "it is not meant for me." But Scripture is clear: "Whatever you do, in word or deed, do everything in the name of the Lord Jesus, giving thanks to God the Father through him" (Col 3:17). Every Christian must seek to serve God and their neighbor in whatever they are doing, whether they have chosen it or it has been forced upon them. This is the point of Paul's "household codes," and it is their ruling principle (Eph 5:22; Col 3:18, 1 Tim 2:8; Titus 2:22). A slave of Christ is a slave all the time and in every relationship, whether marriage, family, or at work.

---

10. Ramelli, *Social Justice*, 177–79.
11. Ramelli, *Social Justice*, 124.
12. Ramelli, *Social Justice*, 2.
13. Ramelli, *Social Justice*, 21.

How Can Slavery Be a Good Thing?

Looked at another way, we could say that all Christian ethics or codes of conduct are determined by our desire to imitate God (1 Cor 11:1; Eph 5:1). God seeks only the good of his creatures. He sacrifices all for our good, helps the helpless, graciously forgives sinners, makes us heirs of heaven. Paul says that we should "have the same attitude that Christ Jesus had. Though he possessed the nature of God, he did not grasp at equality with God but laid it aside to take on the nature of a slave" (Phil 2:5–7, Goodspeed's translation).[14] He did not come to be served but to serve and to give his life as a ransom for many (Mark 10:45). And Jesus expects us to imitate this: "By this all people will know that you are my disciples, if you have love for one another" (John 13:35; see also vv. 12–17). This is why all is done in the "name of the Lord Jesus."

Milton Terry, in his classic book on biblical interpretation written shortly after the Civil War (1883) and still in use today, might consider such general guidelines as these as what he called the "analogy of the faith." It "rests not upon explicit declarations, but upon the obvious scope and import of the Scripture teachings taken as a whole."[15] Terry then makes slavery the prime example of this rule, noting there is no command against it, but when considering the many passages that urge us to love our neighbor as ourselves, "we can scarcely doubt that the holding of any fellow being in bondage against his will is essentially contrary to the highest ethics."[16] This is quite a shift from Hodge's position on slavery before the Civil War.

J. Albert Harrill does not explain this shift, however, as coming from a better understanding of Scripture. He sees the antislavery movement in America as having nothing to do with principles derived from the Bible. In fact, he claims that the best biblical argument was always on the proslavery side. Scripture, he says, obviously allows slavery, and it teaches the subordination of others under authority, both of which can be used to defend slavery. Instead, he sees the antislavery movement as a victory of "moral intuition over the literal words of Scripture."[17] By "moral intuition" he means our natural sense of right and wrong, what some would call "natural law." As we shall see, natural law is what should determine policy, but it is not inconsistent with Scripture. He thinks the rejection of slavery was a victory for higher criticism, which allows you to reject parts of the Bible as being

---

14. Goodspeed, *Bible*, 186.
15. Terry, *Biblical Hermeneutics*, 580.
16. Terry, *Biblical Hermeneutics*, 581.
17. Harrill, *Slaves in the New Testament*, 165.

Part 1: Some "Issues"

historically conditioned and so can be ignored by modern people.[18] In fact, he claims that the same conflict of moral intuition with a literal interpretation of the Bible is still with us. "Biblical literalism versus moral intuition remains at odds in American culture shaping contemporary debate over race relations, military conflict, capital punishment, poverty, abortion, full emancipation of women and lesbian and gay rights."[19] In these conflicts, he believes our "moral intuition" will shape the way we read our Bibles and not the other way around, just as it did with slavery.[20]

Harrill is, I think, right to point out the fact that people do try to use the Bible like a "wax nose" that can be twisted to defend seemingly any moral position. But the Bible is not a "wax nose." Harrill raises an important issue: what is biblical literalism, and is it in favor of slavery? The literal meaning of a text is that meaning which the original writer intended for the original reader. What I think it means may be of some interest, but it may not be what the writer meant to say. It is what the writer meant to say that we are after. Normally, we understand someone's words in context—their context, not ours. Only then can we respond to it intelligently. This is the basis of all clear communication. What is true of everyday conversation is especially true of understanding what God says. An interpreter must be careful not to inject anything subjective or personal into his interpretation. And that is often where problems develop. We bring our own presuppositions and worldview to the text and make it agree with these. This is not literal interpretation.

The original writers and their audience believed that the Bible was a revelation from God (1 Cor 2:13–14), mediated through chosen writers in simple, intelligible words and concepts guided by God's Holy Spirit (2 Tim 3:16). This revelation accurately recorded real events (2 Pet 1:16–21) so that we can know that we are saved by God's grace through faith in Jesus (John 20:31). This was the context of the authors and of their audience. We must use this context, their words, their history, and the logic and grammar of their language to understand what we read.

The written context of the Bible, however, is larger than just the book we happen to be reading. If inspiration is true, the Holy Spirit is the primary author of all Scripture, and we can use what he has written through all the various writers of the Bible in all ages to understand any given text. That

---

18. Harrill, *Slaves in the New Testament*, 174–77.
19. Harrill, *Slaves in the New Testament*, 192.
20. Harrill, *Slaves in the New Testament*, 192.

How Can Slavery Be a Good Thing?

is why we can use cross-references, and why Terry can use "the analogy of faith" to help us understand a text. This is what Christians mean when they say they use "Scripture to interpret Scripture." What St. Augustine, Aquinas, Luther, Calvin, or anyone else says a text may mean is not interpretation. Their opinions may indeed be helpful and even correct, or they may not, but we can only be sure of a thing by what the Bible itself says ("Scripture alone" in Lutheran speak). If we come to Scripture with this kind of humility, we are practicing "literal" interpretation.

When considering passages about slavery, the context then must include 1 Cor 10:23–24. Does it honor God and is it good for the neighbor? This provides not only the rule for dealing with all *adiaphora*, but it creates the "highest moral standard" in dealing with all people. It is true that the Bible accepts the existence of slavery in a fallen world, but it is also true that the Bible requires those who follow Jesus to live by a different standard. Followers of Jesus are to live under the rule of grace, that is, to forget oneself and sacrifice for the good of others just as Jesus did for us. Slavery may be "permissible" (1 Cor 10:23 NIV) in the laws of a fallen world, but it is not "permissible" for a slave of Christ. Philemon must treat his slave as a brother no matter what the law considers him to be (Phlm 16).

It is a historical fact that those Christians who took their Bible quite literally, not those who considered it historically conditioned, eventually spearheaded the movement to make slavery illegal. If you are a Christian who is not bothered by obedience and can pick and choose which things in the Bible apply to you, then none of this need apply to you and you will do as you like. But a slave of Christ must look out "for the good of others," as God has done for us, not condoning evil but working to free people from it (Rom 13:1–10). William Wilberforce in England and the better abolitionists in America, such as Fredrick Douglas, were examples of people who held to a literal understanding of Scripture.

Harrill is right to point out that the Bible teaches respect and obedience to authorities and therefore could be used to defend a slave-like relationship. But, as with 1 Cor 10:23–24, the larger context of Scripture also shows us that this rule has its limits as well. In Acts 5 the apostles practice civil disobedience. Ignoring the command of the authorities, they break the law by continuing to talk about Jesus in public. "We must obey God rather than men" (Acts 5:29). The "must" is because we are first and foremost slaves of Christ, and obedience to his authority must come before all other authorities. It was for this reason that some American Christians ignored the fugitive slave laws and created an "underground railroad" to help African American slaves to freedom in the North and in Canada. Of course, when Christians practice civil disobedience because of their faith, they must be willing to suffer the consequences and the wrath of the authorities. They may become martyrs ("witnesses"). Though, if they do, it will not be as martyrs for a cause but for the one whom they serve even to the point of death.

Before we leave the topic of *adiaphora*, it might be helpful to look at some other things that have been considered *adiaphora* and see how the Bible applies the same rule of faith to them. Most of these involve crossing a line, a natural limit, that results in evil and harm to myself and others. I must not only personally avoid these things, but I must also do what I can to limit the damage they can do. In doing this, however, I must be careful to use only proper lawful action and persuasion (see below on working for change). Despotism, using the force of a dictator, remember, is not a tool we can use. Absolute power belongs only to God, who rules his people through his word and lawfully constituted government (Rom 13:1–7). In seeking limits on the evils of this world we have the example of Scripture itself. Scripture may not forbid certain "dangerous" things, and the list of these things could be potentially very large, but it does often give warnings and restrictions for the wise (those who want to honor God) to follow.

Gambling may not be a sin per se, e.g., the fun of playing a game of chance. But if it leads to greed (Col 3:5), to addiction and crime, or if it takes advantage of people, especially the poor, then it crosses the line into sin. Drinking alcohol or using other legal drugs is not a sin. Jesus even provided wine for a wedding feast (John 2:1–12), and Paul told Timothy to take a little wine for his stomach (1 Tim 5:23). But if it leads to drunkenness (impairment) or addiction, it crosses the line into sin (Eph 5:18; 1 Cor 6:10). Though the use of a medically prescribed drug may be legal and helpful, substance abuse destroys our health and relationships (1 Cor 10:23–24). Polygamy may be in some places a legal and accepted practice, as in Old Testament times, but since it is not God's intention for marriage (monogamy, Gen 2:24), and because it is often abusive to women and can cause great suffering in the family, the Bible places strong restrictions on it among God's people (Exod 21:10; Deut 17:17; 21:15–17). Divorce may not be sinful when used to protect a life (Matt 19:9; 1 Cor 7:15), but since it is often caused by the sin of a "hard heart" (Matt 19:3–9), it becomes abusive, especially to women and children, and crosses the line into sin (Deut 24:1–4;

Matt 19:9). Notice that all these things may or may not become dangerous physically and spiritually to you and others, but when something leads to sin, it is not "indifferent" any longer. You are not free to use them any way you want.

It is never wise to assume God is indifferent about something simply because he appears to be silent on the issue. It may just be that you don't want to listen. Those who want to justify an evil by calling it an *adiaphoron* should listen carefully to Ps 50:16–22 (NIV):

> What right have you to recite my laws or take my covenant on your lips? You hate my instruction and cast my words behind you. When you see a thief, you join with him; you throw in your lot with adulterers. You use your mouth for evil and harness your tongue to deceit. You sit and testify against your brother and slander your own mother's son. When you did these things and I kept silent, you thought I was exactly like you. But I now arraign you and set my accusations before you. Consider this, you who forget God, or I will tear you to pieces, with no one to rescue you.

In this fallen world we can find many things that are unwise, stupid, foolish, and can lead to sin. If we are to be wise, we must remember that "the fear of the Lord is the beginning of wisdom" (Ps 111:10; Prov 1:7). Fear means not only to fear making him angry, as above, but also to hold him in highest respect and honor. Without the fear of his justice, we would not appreciate his mercy. These are two sides of the same coin. God is both just and merciful, and so we both fear and love him. Johann Gerhard, the seventeenth-century theologian, put it this way: "The fear of God is to be united with the love of God; for love without fear makes men remiss, and fear without love makes them servile and desperate."[21] And so, Luther puts them together in his explanation of every commandment, "We should fear and love God so that we . . ."[22]

This is why slavery to Christ is neither "servile and desperate" (like human slavery) nor is it "remiss" (as with those who ignore obedience to God). God is to be first in our lives, the highest authority and highest value, because of the great mercy he has shown us in Jesus (Rom 12:1–2). This is why we listen to God's warnings throughout Scripture—not only because we don't want to make him angry but because we love him and we want to please him in everything we do (Col 3:17). We trust him to know what is

---

21. Keil and Delitzsch, *Commentary*, 1:343.
22. Luther, Luther's Small Catechism, 13.

best for us. To always do what will please God and to avoid that which hurts and destroys us and others is to live wisely (2 Cor 5:9; 2 Tim 2:4). There is a whole genre in the Bible called wisdom literature that deals with many of life's problems in just this way.

And so, the New Testament gives us wisdom about how to live in a world that may legalize slavery and many other evils. If I find myself in slavery, I must use it to serve God and my neighbor. If I can gain my freedom, I should (1 Cor 7:21) because it will improve my ability to serve God and my neighbor. If I have any influence to legally abolish slavery, I should do so because that too would serve God and my neighbor, rescuing him or her from physical and mental abuse. If I own slaves when I become a Christian, I should treat them like my brothers and sisters (Phlm 16) and work to free them not only legally but by preparing them to live on their own.

Though we are struck by the gracious behavior of some Christians in the first centuries who raised funds to buy their fellow Christians out of slavery, it should probably not surprise us that the early church actually told them to stop doing this.[23] It was causing a violent backlash, and they did not want Christianity to be identified as a social or political movement. The need to serve God by combating social evils, though, has always been a part of the church in every age, even though the time and the place have often redefined what social evils are attacked. In historical context, we must pick and choose our battles, and we may find fault with the choice of those who came before us, but it is never easy to see other people's difficulties clearly, any more than it is to see our own.

C. S. Lewis once gave some rather practical advice to some idealistic Christians who wanted to end all war:

> I have received no assurance that anything we can do will eradicate suffering. I think the best results are obtained by people who work quietly away at limited objectives, such as the abolition of the slave trade, or prison reform, or factory acts, or tuberculosis, not by those who think they can achieve universal justice, or health, or peace. I think the art of life consists in tackling each immediate evil as well as we can. To avert or postpone one particular war by wise policy, or to render one particular campaign shorter by strength and skill or less terrible by mercy to the conquered and the civilians, is more useful than all the proposals for universal peace that have ever been made.[24]

23. Ramelli, *Social Justice*, 2.
24. Lewis, *Weight of Glory*, 44–45.

How Can Slavery Be a Good Thing?

The confusion of rapid change, of having too many options, of not knowing what is really going on around you, as well as the worldview of your culture, make it difficult to choose which "immediate evil" to fight. But these are not excuses. St. Paul writes, "Only let us hold true to what we have attained" (Phil 3:16). We must try to live by those principles from Scripture that are clear to us. Before we look at a Christian's social and political action, though, we must consider other ways Christians have dealt with slavery in the past other than as an *adiaphoron*.

Other Views of Slavery

Americans are most familiar with ethnic slavery and its continuing expressions of prejudice, e.g., white supremacy. Many will also know ethnic slavery has also been defended by some using the Bible. The classic example is Noah's curse of his son Ham in Gen 9:25–26. It is supposed that the descendants of Ham settled in Africa and therefore were meant to be slaves. But the curse is not on Ham at all, but on his son, Canaan. "Cursed be Canaan; a servant of servants shall he be to his brothers" (Gen 9:25). Genesis places the descendants of Ham not in Africa but in the Middle East, from Egypt to Iran. Further, this prophecy specifically refers to the land of Canaan and Israel's conquest of the Canaanites who lived in the Middle East centuries later. It has nothing to do with Africa and nothing to do with race since Genesis knows only one race, the human race (Acts 17:26). The curse of Ham was never applied to Africa until the beginning of the slave trade to the Americas as a twisted justification for slavery.

The ancients did not feel they even needed justification for slavery. It simply always had been, always would be. From their perspective, slavery was normal. If there were wars where your enemies were captured and you had the power or the wealth to make people serve you, there would be slavery. Perhaps they had a point since even though slavery is now commonly against the law throughout the world, slavery still widely exists in sex trafficking, abuse of immigrant labor, sweat shops, and in many other forms. That it exists, however, does not mean that it should exist, nor that we should accept it as the Stoics did.

Then, as now, there were advanced two practical arguments for its existence. There was the "natural" explanation, from Aristotle to Darwin, which says that since people naturally vary in ability and intelligence, slavery is only natural for those on the lower end of the scale. It is a natural way to use their limited abilities while taking care of them since they cannot take very good care of themselves. And then there is the "pragmatic" explanation, from the Stoics to some modern political systems (fascism, communism, etc.). They are willing to say that all people are born free and slavery is "unnatural" in that sense but that societies may employ slavery as a "useful" tool to control the lower classes and keep order in society. Some, like St. Augustine, even saw it as a constructive punishment for evil people (e.g., chain gangs).[25]

There is also a modern Marxist-inspired explanation of slavery called wokism. Wokism is a racist theory (literally, being both about race and racist itself) which blames the existence of slavery and the abuse of former slaves in America on power struggles between races (substituting "race" for the usual Marxist category of "class"). As in the first century, this makes slavery a natural part of the world. It's the way things are—a power game. Just make sure it's the other guy who is the slave. But slavery and the abuse of slaves has had nothing to do with race for most of its history. Greed, hatred, lust for power, fear, and all that comes from the sinful heart are better explanations for the existence and use of slavery, now and in the past.

The Bible's Impact

Even though slavery was universally accepted in the ancient world, we must remember that ideas are powerful, and the distinctive differences in the Judeo-Christian worldview would inevitably come to challenge the understanding and practice of slavery in Western nations.

First and most importantly in this worldview was the Bible's teaching about creation, as we saw in Gregory of Nyssa. It taught that all people came from the same couple, Adam and Eve, and thus are part of the same human family (Acts 17:26–27). We are "created equal," as Jefferson put it in the Declaration of Independence. Job says of his slaves, "Did not he who made me in the womb make them? Did not the same one form us both within our mothers?" (Job 31:13–15 NIV; see also Prov 14:31; 17:5; 29:13). All the descendants of Adam have sinned and deserve death, but Christ has redeemed all people (Rom 3:23–25; 1 Cor 15:22, 45–49) so that Paul can say "there is neither Jew nor Greek, slave nor free . . . for you are all one in Christ" (Gal 3:28 NIV). In the church, if not in society, there was thus already a foundation for change. Christopher Wright observed that in

---

25. de Wet, *Unbound God*, 116–19.

How Can Slavery Be a Good Thing?

the Bible, "Slavery is seen as unnatural, fallen and accursed, in no way an essential and unchangeable part of the 'nature of things.'"[26]

Unlike much of the ancient world, Wright observes that among the Hebrews, slavery was "not regarded as a divinely ordered part of creation itself, as though slave and free were different degrees of humanity."[27] The equality that came from a biblical understanding of the creation of all people in the image of God was distinctive then, as now, and underlies the concept of human rights. Jefferson, in the Declaration of Independence, understood that not only are all men created equal but that because of this, their creator gives all men the rights of life, liberty, and the pursuit of happiness. This became a doctrine of humanism only because Christianity had already planted it in Western culture.

The next important difference in the Judeo-Christian worldview came from the fact that Israel had been slaves in Egypt for four centuries. It was essentially a nation of runaway slaves. Wright observes that "this experience coloured their subsequent attitude to slavery enormously."[28] According to Lev 25, you could not enslave a fellow Israelite for the very practical reason that they already had a master and they were already slaves of God (Lev 25:42). Even though you could temporarily enslave an Israelite for debt, you could not "rule over [them] ruthlessly" (Lev 25:43). Rather "he shall be with you as a hired servant" (Lev 25:40). He is not a hired servant but only to be treated as one. Not only that, but Hebrew slaves were to be released after six years (Deut 15:12–15). You could, however, enslave non-Jews for life (Deut 15:45–46). Still, in Israel, all slaves had rights and protections not found anywhere else in the ancient world.

They were given a day of rest, one day out of seven as a sabbath, which was explicitly said to be also for slaves because Israel had been enslaved (Exod 20:10; 23:12). Slaves could participate in some religious rituals as well (Deut 12:11–12). There were also laws protecting slaves from bodily harm. Exodus 21:20 required that a slave killed by his master was to be "avenged." Although how they were to be avenged is not stated, it is probable that this meant the master could be tried for murder since he had taken a human life (Gen 9:6). Exodus 21:26–27 required that a slave badly injured by his master was to be set free. Jesus, in the Sermon on the Mount, includes all kinds of physical harm and even hate and insults under the

---

26. Wright, *Eye for an Eye*, 182.
27. Wright, *Eye for an Eye*, 182.
28. Wright, *Eye for an Eye*, 179.

fifth commandment; though no reason is given here for either law, it can be seen to reflect the very Hebrew idea of the sanctity of human life. At the very least, such rules protecting slaves are a tacit recognition of the evil of slavery and the slave as a person with some rights under the law.

The most unique slave law in Israel was the law of asylum in Deut 15:16. A runaway slave, far from being sent back and punished, as would have happened in Greece or Rome, was to be given freedom of residence in a village set aside for this, called a city of refuge. That a slave was allowed to run away from an abusive master may also have come from Israel's history. The Jews had experienced God as sympathetic to runaway slaves. Christopher Wright even identifies this as an important theme of Scripture: "God wants nothing more but that we run away from our abusive masters of sin and hell to a city of refuge in his kingdom, to find a new home with a new and loving master."[29]

In that regard, we should also note that the word "slave" does not carry negative connotations when used in the Bible of our relationship with God. This difference when speaking about our relationship with God can also be seen in how the Bible speaks about the concept of jealousy. Stopping for comment in the middle of the Ten Commandments, God says, "I the LORD your God am a jealous God" (Exod 20:5). Most people would think that jealousy is a bad thing. It describes being hurt and angry when you think someone is trying to take what is rightfully yours. It is a form of possessiveness. A jealous boyfriend may attack someone who shows interest in his girlfriend because he thinks, "That girl belongs to me!" But this kind of jealousy is always wrong (1 Cor 3:3; Gal 5:19–20), and those who belong to God know that no human being can belong to another human being.

However, when this word is applied to God, the situation is changed. As our creator, we are his possession, and he is within his rights to be possessive and insist that we honor and serve him. He is rightly jealous. The same can be said of slavery. When one human being owns another, it is always wrong, and for the same reason. No human being can belong to another. But when that word is used of God, the situation is changed. When God owns us and we belong to him, everything is as it should be. Being a slave of God only describes the reality of who and what we are as his creatures. But slavery is a good thing only when you have the right master.

The Bible expresses a dignified view of humanity. We are created in the image of God. It expresses an equality under the law of God—equally helpless to save ourselves, equally redeemed by the blood of Christ, freely given

---

29. Wright, *Eye for an Eye*, 181.

to all who believe. We are then to live equally with all, showing respect to those who bear the image of God. Christianity has been the driving force in the abolition of many restrictions on human freedoms—in human rights, politics and government, women's rights, child labor, prisons, and slavery. Its influence has been, admittedly, uneven and inconsistent throughout history, for as it became a powerful cultural institution, it often promoted the status quo over the teachings of the Bible, as we noted.

But when we go back to the first centuries, those early Christians tried to largely ignore social class (Jas 2:1-13), race, and all worldly categories (Gal 3:28). For this reason, those who identified as slaves of Christ were the humblest of people, accepting those from all social classes as equals (Acts 2:42-47). There were glitches, as with the suspicion between the Hebrew and the Greek Christians (Acts 6:1), but the point is that the apostles did not accept this but set about to correct it. Even though the world's standards would continue to find their way into the church, this understanding of the value and equality of humanity would continue to survive and grow in various ways.

There are different ways that ideas survive and grow in a society, but I think it is important for Christians to understand how they can best work for these changes. Ideas of the worth and equality of slaves were not forced on people—not even by our Civil War and by a constitutional amendment. More than a hundred years later we still struggle with civil rights for the descendants of ex-slaves. Ideas cannot be forced. They must be "caught" from people who not only believe them but who also live by them. Evils that are "permissible" or "lawful" are not simply to be accepted by the people of God. We are not Stoics. We must work for God-pleasing change. This responsibility means that Christians must be involved in some form of social and political action in their societies. But this is where the church is most likely to be misunderstood, as I noted in the introduction, as nothing but a political organization with a social agenda. "Slaves of Christ," for example, could be seen as a banner, a slogan, or rally point for a politically active group like a "Christian Democratic Party" found in some countries. But this must not be. And here is why.

How Things Change

The New Testament kingdom of God, unlike the Old Testament kingdom, is not a theocracy, where the church rules the state. Jesus said his kingdom was "not of this world" and did not control territory or use military force like worldly kingdoms (John 18:36). He said his kingdom consists of those who "listen to his voice"—people of every nation, under all forms of government, who believe and follow the word of God (John 18:37). People are persuaded by hearing that voice in God's word where the Spirit of God works, not by force but by changing hearts (Rom 10:14–17; 2 Cor 5:11). As Michael Card observed, Jesus "is not a social reformer. He is a person reformer."[30] The Bible's main concern is with individuals who are sinners separated from God and reconciled to God through faith, one by one. Therefore, the greater the number of individuals who become followers of Christ and seek to serve him, the more likely society will be influenced by these people. If the Bible has any political or social philosophy, it is the philosophy of the old proverb: "For the forest to be green, the trees must be green." In other words, it's by changing enough individuals into followers of Jesus that you change society. Sharing the good news of Jesus must always be our first priority, and that will always be the best and surest way of changing society, but that does not excuse us from our responsibility of serving our neighbor in their physical life as well (Jas 2:15–17). And so we must talk about our responsibilities as Christians in two "kingdoms," in the church and in the state.

According to the New Testament, Christians are to "render to Caesar the things that are Caesar's, and to God the things that are God's" (Matt 22:21). Paul taught that the government has control over the physical lives of its citizens and can use force to keep law and order (Rom 13:1–7). The church, on the other hand, has responsibility over the spiritual life of its people and uses the teaching of God's word to create and sustain faith in Jesus and willing obedience to him (John 18:36; 20:21–23; 2 Cor 10:4–5). This principle was clearly stated as early as AD 355 by Bishop Hosius of Cordova, who was at that time more powerful than the bishop of Rome.[31] He and Martin of Tours strongly objected when the emperor began executing heretics because the church was to respond to false teaching with right teaching, not force. The temptation to use force, however, won out.[32]

There are religions that believe that the church should rule over the state and use force to do so. For a time, the Christian church had great political power in the late Roman Empire through the Middle Ages, but today Islam would be a better example of this practice. It could be argued

---

30. Card, *Better Freedom*, 54.
31. Davies, *Early Christian Church*, 163.
32. Davies, *Early Christian Church*, 164.

that the power struggles between church and state in the West slowed its missionary expansion into Europe while the church in the East, in the Persian Empire and China, never had any political power, and yet it almost succeeded in quickly making Christianity the dominant religion of Asia.[33] It was only prevented by the rapid rise of Islam in the 700s, which had no qualm in using force to promote its religion. Islam, however, soon tore itself into warring factions which continue to this day. When the state wants to control minds or the church wants to make laws, the results are usually painful. In modern times the West has largely developed the practice of a "separation of powers" between church and state.

During the Reformation, Luther rejected the idea of the church using the force of government.[34] Luther called it a "separation of powers" and not "a separation of church and state" because he believed that both church and state were to use their separate powers to serve God's purposes in the world. They were to work together as God's left and right hands in the world, to cooperate as much as possible without confusing their separate responsibilities. Consequently, when Christians deal with the state, we are to remember that government makes laws for the whole community, both Christians and non-Christians. Non-Christians have no reason to accept the authority or the directives of God's word. Even though civil law should not deal with matters of faith, it must deal with matters of how we treat each other. Although Christians will accept the Bible's authority in these matters, non-Christians will not.

God's moral law, however, is, as Paul says, "written on the hearts" of all people because of their creation in the image of God and is found in their conscience (Rom 2:14–20).[35] Most people have a commonsense view of right and wrong, usually called "natural law." It is what seems "fair," "seems right," "makes sense" to "reasonable" people. Christians, informed by God's perfect law, must appeal in political/legal contexts, not to Scripture but to reason, logic, and common sense. This is why persuasion is our only weapon in politics and government. This doesn't mean we can't use our power to vote for desired change or appeal to existing law to get the government to do what is right, and it certainly doesn't mean we can't quote Scripture. It only means that quoting Scripture won't convince most people of anything

---

33. Frankopan, *Silk Road*, 54–61.

34. Luther, "Temporal Authority," 75–129.

35. C. S. Lewis has termed this universal moral sense the "Tao" and describes it, and what happens when we ignore it, in his book *Abolition of Man*.

and we must reason with and persuade people to change, even when we don't feel we should have to.

Contrary to how we are portrayed in the media, Christians are not out to punish, imprison, and kill those who disagree with them. We are commanded to "overcome evil with good" (Rom 12:9–21). We are not trying to take over the government or trying to "brain wash" or force people to think the way we do. Our only tool is persuasion. "For the weapons of our warfare are not of the flesh but have divine power to destroy strongholds. We destroy arguments and every lofty opinion raised against the knowledge of God" (2 Cor 10:4–5). We use our words and the example of our lives to influence others. We also influence the political process with our values, in so far as any political system allows input from its citizens, using public speech and votes. We have as much right to such influence as anyone. Christian individuals must be involved in politics to protect and serve our neighbor. But that does not mean we are free to use any of the methods used in modern politics, especially the modern trend of labeling and attacking people instead of dealing honestly with their positions.

Persuasion works best through relationships, and so is most effective when done, as Peter says, with "gentleness and respect" (1 Pet 3:15). As a tool for influencing people, for example, we should note the subtle difference between a demonstration and protest. They may not be clearly distinguished, but protest implies an angry attack on a person or policy. A demonstration, on the other hand, implies a peaceful attempt to focus on a needed change. Christians should be careful to demonstrate the reason for needed change and its importance. Protest creates pushback and adversarial relationships. When slaves protest, they get crucified. When Christians protest, Christianity can get crucified. It is because of protest that many people know more about what Christians are against than what they are for. It has led many people to think of Christians as negative, judgmental, and hateful—and why they want nothing to do with Christianity.

It is better to seek a respectful relationship with those with whom we disagree in which we listen, ask them the difficult questions, and respond thoughtfully to their positions. We may not be treated the same way. Others may shout at us, but that does not give us permission to shout back in return (Rom 12:17). Slaves of Christ are to humbly practice self-control and not let themselves be mastered by anger, fear, or a need to win. Our master is the Spirit of Christ (Gal 5:19–24; Ezek 2:6; Jer 1:8; 2 Tim 1:7). If we truly represent Christ, we can trust Christ to be in control of the outcomes. We are only to be faithful and obedient to say what is right and do what is right with gentleness and respect. We must be careful to demonstrate why we do what we do and explain the reasons behind it. This is much harder than protesting or saying that Scripture is against it, but it will have better results.

When Jesus said, "Let your light shine before others, so that they may see your good works and give glory to your Father who is in heaven" (Matt 5:16), he must have meant also explaining why we do what we do. We must talk about Jesus and our love for him as the reason for what we do. Otherwise, people will think we are just trying to be good, like people do in every other religion. How would they know our words and actions come from our love of Jesus? How would they end up giving glory to our Father who is in heaven instead of giving credit or glory to you for being "nice?" Christians who are not open about following Jesus and their reasons for what they do are only adding to misunderstanding and the slide of our culture into a new paganism.

If we care about people, we will want to help them and share with them the good news about Jesus and the other truths of Scripture, even while we are using reason and natural law to persuade. Peter says we must do this "with gentleness and respect." This does not mean we cannot be firm in our position. Still, if you disagree with some people, they will automatically think you are attacking them, so we will need to be as clear and as kind as possible, even though continuing to firmly disagree. Jesus did this (John 4:7–29). It is often possible to disagree without being disagreeable, but we can only do what we can do. As Paul said, " So far as it depends on you, live peaceably with all" (Rom 12:18). But it does not always depend on us. Jesus clashed with others too (Matt 23:1–36). But what we can do, we must do.

John Dickson, in his guide to world religions, criticizes our culture's idea of "pluralism"—a belief that all religions are different paths to the same truth. He has some wonderful advice about how to disagree. He disagrees with pluralism. How can you know that all religions lead to the same place? Every religion would disagree not only with that claim but with the truth claims of every other religion. You cannot wish the differences away. But you can at least do them the honor of taking them each seriously. He writes:

> Tolerance does not mean that we should try to accept each other's beliefs as true or as equally valid perceptions.... That would involve turning off the part of the brain that tries to avoid contradiction.... I love what the great early-twentieth-century English

author and public intellectual G. K. Chesterton once said about this.... "If I think the universe is triangular, and you think it is square, there cannot be room for two universes. We may argue politely, we may argue humanely, we may argue with great mutual benefit; but, obviously, we must argue. Modern toleration is really a tyranny. It is a tyranny because it is a silence. To say that I must not deny my opponent's faith is to say I must not discuss it." This way of thinking about tolerance—as the pursuit of agreement—is doomed to fail. But there is a more sensible and workable definition of tolerance. True tolerance is the noble ability to treat with respect and friendship those with whom we deeply disagree.... The real humanitarian spirit is found in being able to love those with whom we profoundly disagree.[36]

We must not avoid, and we must not attack; we must serve. That should be what a slave of Christ does best.

---

36. Dickson, *Doubter's Guide*, 293–95.

TAKEAWAY

In this section we have considered some issues in our world that may prevent us from understanding what it means to be a slave of Christ. First, we had to confront our problems with obedience. These problems come especially from philosophies and worldviews that have developed since the Enlightenment. Many are self-centered and materialistic and have no place for obedience. The influence of cheap grace and Moralistic Therapeutic Deism have given us freedom from God instead of freedom from sin. Real freedom is only possible when we have Jesus as our master. Not all obedience is legalism, and it does not conflict with salvation by grace alone but flows naturally from it. We must not withdraw from the world but engage it as his faithful people. Has it been one of your goals to be obedient to Jesus? Do you ever think about this? If not, why not?

There is a danger in thinking of "slave of Christ" as just a metaphor. This often allows us to dismiss the radical claim that Christ has on us—on our bodies, our obedience, our minds ("take every thought captive to obey Christ," 2 Cor 10:5). This slavery is quite literal. We are saint and sinner at the same time, and we should especially note that in Rom 6 the saint or new man is also a slave of Christ. As Luther explained in his *Freedom of the Christian*, we are freed from sin and death by the love of Christ for us, and, in return, we freely serve those around us out of love for Christ, a new and different kind of bondage. To understand real freedom, it helps to be firmly grounded in reality, that is, in a biblical worldview. Would you say your worldview is consistent with your faith? Where are you most inconsistent? Does the kind of freedom presented here seem like freedom to you? Why or why not?

It may bother some people that the New Testament does not explicitly forbid slavery, but it certainly does not advocate or defend it either. The institution was a reality of first-century life to be used by the slave as an opportunity to glorify God. At the same time, Christians were to live very differently within a slave society. Philemon is to take back his runaway slave and treat him as a brother in Christ, not as piece of property (Phlm 16). Slavery does not qualify as an *adiaphoron*, an "indifferent" thing, since we have clear directives against using things which are not for the good of others (1 Cor 10:23–24). It simply does not agree with Scripture's view of humanity, God's right of ownership as creator, or the command to love our neighbor. These truths make human slavery a kind of idolatry. What do you think of the way Christians have dealt with slavery in the past? What lessons can we learn from that in confronting new evils? How can conflict be an opportunity to glorify God?

We must be careful, however, in the way we use Scripture to change our society and its laws. As citizens, we must do what we can to create just laws using natural law, reason, and persuasion, but as Christians, our job is to change hearts with God's word. In the end, that will prove the best way to change a society. Do you think that politics and social involvement is a way to serve your neighbor? Why or why not? What are you involved in now, or what do you think you should be involved in? Is it a witness to your faith? Would others agree?

PART 2
Belonging

"But you are a chosen race, a royal priesthood, a holy nation, a people for his own possession, that you may proclaim the excellencies of him who called you out of darkness into his marvelous light. Once you were not a people, but now you are God's people; once you had not received mercy, but now you have received mercy." —1 PETER 2:9–10

CHAPTER 4

What Does It Mean to Belong?

"You are Christ's."—1 CORINTHIANS 3:23

IN HIS *SMALL CATECHISM*, Luther teaches us to say: "I believe that Jesus . . . is my Lord, who has redeemed me, a lost and condemned person, purchased and won me from all sins, from death, and from the power of the devil; not with gold or silver, but with his holy, precious blood and with his innocent suffering and death, *that I may be his own and live under him in his kingdom and serve him in everlasting righteousness, innocence, and blessedness.*"[1] We are bought by Jesus. We belong to Jesus. We serve him only. We are his slaves. That is simply what Luther thought a Christian was.

A slave is, first of all then, someone who has been purchased and belongs to another. We have already seen that belonging to God is different than one human being belonging to another, but how is it different? To the Romans a slave was a *res*, a *mancipium*, a thing that could be owned, but also a *res mortales*, a mortal or living thing, "chattel"—the same legal category as cattle or sheep.[2] Legally a slave was "fungible property" (an object that could be exchanged for something of equal value, like money, grain, cattle, or some other object) and nothing more. But being an intelligent animal, a slave's relationship with his or her owner was often much more complicated. Even though a slave had no legal rights, their master might allow them more freedom, wealth, and power than a nobleman—or not. They could be treated as an object, or as an equal, and anything in between,

---

1. Luther, Luther's Small Catechism, 17. Emphasis added.
2. Crook, *Law and Life of Rome*, 55–56.

depending on their master. Everything depends on who you belong to, as we shall see.

There are many contexts that can help us understand the relationship of belonging. We could define "belonging" legally as a matter of property rights and power over another. Or we could define it relationally or interpersonally by how one is valued and treated by another. Or we could define it behaviorally by what one is allowed to do and not do, or by how much freedom of choice one has. All of these are important ways to help us understand belonging, and therefore, in this chapter, we shall consider how Scripture deals with each. As slaves of Christ, we are legally defined by our creation—made by him, we belong to him (1 Pet 2:9). Almost like the Roman concept of chattel, we are also "the sheep of his pasture" (Ps 100:3). Behaviorally we are defined by having Jesus as our king (John 18:33–37). We "live under him in his kingdom and serve him"—we are expected to obey our king and do what he says. In this relationship we are the subjects of a benevolent king and so enjoy many benefits along with the responsibilities. Relationally, however, we are defined as family—he is our father; we are his *familia*.

The Roman concept of *familia*, as in most ancient families, includes all those in the household who were under the authority of the *pater familia*.[3] This effectively puts everyone in the family under the absolute authority and power of the father. Every member of the family was in some sense a slave to the father. As such, we can then find ourselves in every relationship within the family. We are the bride of Christ (Eph 5:22–33), the children of God (1 John 3:1–2), brothers and sisters of Christ (Mark 3:34–35), and slaves of Christ (Luke 17:7–10). In the Roman world, slaves were considered a part of the household, members of the *familia*. Their identity came from the family they belonged to. If freed by a Roman citizen, for example, they became a Roman citizen listed under the *gens* or name of the family that freed them and with all the family obligations that came with it.[4] As it turns out, it makes very little practical difference which position we hold since all are under the same authority, whether slave or free.

Children are born into a family not only as a child of parents but also as a sibling, as a brother or sister (as Christians have always referred to each other). Birth, the creation of a new person, can put someone into all these relationships, even slave; therefore, we will deal especially with birth

---

3. Andreau and Descat, *Slave in Greece and Rome*, 68.
4. Andreau and Descat, *Slave in Greece and Rome*, 152.

What Does It Mean to Belong?

in a separate chapter where we discuss baptism as a way of being born into God's family. We shall consider each of the other household members who are under the authority of the *pater familia* in the chapter on service. For now, since most families begin with marriage, with husbands and wives, as our first family did (Gen 2:22–24), that will be the first relationship we will look at more closely. Since marriage is clearly a relation of persons, not things (*res*), it will, for that reason also, be a good place to start.

Marriage

Marriage is a common way God describes his relationship with the church in both the Old and New Testaments, but it is not a term used to describe individuals. No one person can say they are *the* bride of Christ or *a* bride of Christ. It is meant to describe the church, the whole group of Christians, as one body. Still, we can apply the idea personally, that is, to one who belongs to this church, because generally what applies to the class applies to every member of the class. Being part of the group, we share the characteristics of the group.

The Christian church is described as the "bride of Christ" (Eph 5:25–32; Rev 19:6–9) because, as in the ancient marriage rite, when Christ returns, he will, like the bridegroom, claim his bride and take her home to live with him. God's covenant with his faithful people, based on the forgiveness of sins, is often described by God as a marriage covenant. If people leave him for other gods, it is said to be "adultery" or even "whoring" after other gods (Jer 3:6–12). These words can describe not only the group but also the individuals in that group who worship other gods.

But what does marriage have to do with belonging? St. Paul uses marriage to describe our belonging to Jesus:

> For a married woman is bound by law to her husband while he lives, but if her husband dies she is released from the law of marriage. Accordingly, she will be called an adulteress if she lives with another man while her husband is alive. But if her husband dies, she is free from that law, and if she marries another man, she is not an adulteress. Likewise, my brothers, you also have died to the law through the body of Christ, so that you may *belong to another*, to him who has been raised from the dead, in order that we may bear fruit for God. (Rom 7:2–4, emphasis added)

Part 2: Belonging

We tend to think that marriage is just about love. You know, "love and marriage go together like a horse and carriage" sort of thing. The cynical among us may even think of it as an economic arrangement, or even a sexual one. But the distinctive thing about marriage is not love, sex, or economics, but belonging. People can love each other, financially support, have sex with, or even lay down their lives for another without being married to them. But in the biblical view of marriage, a man and a woman will do all these things for each other because they belong to each other; they have become part of one new creature. They have become "one flesh" (Gen 2:24).

Married people take responsibility for each other and for any children they have, and to this common end, they share resources: "What's mine is yours, what's yours is mine." In 1 Cor 7:4 Paul teaches that the husband's body belongs to the wife and that the wife's body belongs to her husband, a principle that doesn't stop with sexual union. In Eph 5 a husband and wife are called upon to sacrifice anything for their common good. It helps if you are in love, but the real blessing of marriage is that you belong to each other. "Bone of my bones and flesh of my flesh," said Adam (Gen 2:23). Adam and Eve were married the day they met. They didn't get married because they loved each other; they loved each other because they were married.

If marriage is belonging to each other, then other than this, there are only two other possible ways to understand belonging in marriage:

1. Marriage could be where only one person belongs to another—marriage as slavery. For thousands of years marriage was understood to mean the woman belonged to the man, end of story. One person belonging to another is, as we have seen, the wrong kind of slavery. Sometimes these marriages did become as abusive as other forms of human slavery—though, to be fair, there were many happy marriages too. And although Paul seems to be referring to this kind of marriage above, emphasizing God's claim on us, this does not rule out our resulting claim on him. At any rate, we must remember that slavery to God is the only right kind of slavery.

2. Alternately, there is what is now considered the cure for marriage as slavery where no one belongs to anyone. Everyone is free to come and go as they like. This could be called "living together" or "an open marriage" or even "ethical non-monogamy" which many people now consider to be a new and improved form of marriage. In this arrangement, I have no claim on you, and you have no claim on me. Two

people use each other to meet their financial, sexual, and emotional needs until that isn't working any more or someone better comes along. Using each other, even by mutual agreement, might be the definition of an abusive relationship but not of marriage.[5] Still, this is how many modern people try to guard against marriage becoming a form of slavery. Of course, it doesn't work. It is only another form of using people as objects (*res*), another form of abuse, another kind of slavery.

There is a better way: the model of marriage that Jesus used when he compared himself to a bridegroom, that is, marriage where two people belong to each other, share all in common, become one. In several parables Jesus describes himself as the bridegroom who will come and claim those who trust in him, his bride, and take them to heaven to share his home with them, e.g., Matt 25:1–13. In Revelation, heaven is even described as "the wedding feast of the Lamb" (Rev 19:6–10). In the Old Testament God describes himself as the bridegroom and Israel, his faithful people, as his bride (Isa 62:1–5). Why? Because just as in marriage, our relationship with God is about belonging.

Like a groom, God claims us and makes us his own. He did this even though we were not worth having.[6] Still, as with a wedding, he not only takes us to himself but also gives himself to us. Remember "what's mine is yours, what's yours is mine?" We share with him what is ours: our debt of sin, our lack of righteousness, our disobedience, our sentence of death, our future hell, and Jesus takes all this as if it were his own. And Jesus shares with us what is his: his perfection, righteousness, obedience to the Father, his life surrendered on a cross to pay our debt, and his home in heaven. What belongs to us belongs to him. What belongs to him belongs to us. He will sacrifice everything for our good, like the perfect husband of Eph 5:25, so that we can have all that belongs to him.

In the psalms, phrases like "God is my portion forever" (Ps 73:26) is the Old Testament way of expressing my claim on him. Since he has graciously given himself to me so that I may live with him forever, he is my eternal possession (Gen 15:1). The inverse is, of course, also true: "The LORD's portion is his people, Jacob his allotted heritage" (Deut 32:9). We belong to each other. "I am my beloved's, and my beloved is mine" (Song 6:3). Often

---

5. Not surprisingly, it shares some aspects of the Roman practical business view of marriage. Crook, *Law and Life of Rome*, 99–106.

6. In the book of Hosea, God has Hosea marry a prostitute to show God's faithfulness to a faithless people.

in the psalms the idea is expressed that even if I have nothing else in this life, having him is all I need.

But there is at least one more way that our relationship with God is like marriage—the now and the not yet quality of the relationship. Marriage takes place in an instant, in a "now," in an event called a wedding ceremony ("I take you to be . . . I pronounce you to be . . ."). From that moment on everything is changed. "I" cease to exist, and "we" begin, a new creation. From that moment everything I have belongs to my wife and everything she has is mine. In the same way, faith is born in a moment, and whether it is at baptism or at some other point, it is a moment in time, and in that moment, we receive all that belongs to Jesus, salvation is ours, and he receives all that is ours. We belong to him. We call this justification. But after that moment comes the rest of life. After the wedding comes the marriage. The difficult changes and sacrifices made for the other are just beginning. The marriage is also a "not yet." It is not easy to live in a new relationship, to make all the changes this new relationship requires. We call this sanctification. Marriage is sometimes called a "school for Christian character" because it requires us to learn how to stop thinking only of ourselves and to bend for another, to give and sacrifice, just as Christ did for us.

In the same way, after the moment in which faith is born, after the wedding, the marriage continues. Then comes life with Christ, in which, like a good husband, he continues to share all his gifts with us. He will lead us, teach us, challenge our faithfulness, and strengthen our faith so that we confess him as Lord until he takes us to his home in heaven. He even gives us spiritual gifts (Eph 4:7–12; 1 Cor 12:27–31). The catch is that these gifts are not really *for* us. They are given *to* us, but we are to use them *for* others. As in marriage, everything is sacrificed for the common good of the family (1 Cor 12:7; 1 Pet 4:10). All things are shared to meet the needs of others. As we shall see in the next section on serving, like a good steward, a slave of Christ receives everything from his master and shares it, serving Christ by serving others. The pattern of receiving and serving is as deeply embedded in the marriage relationship as it is in our relationship with God (Eph 5:25).

There is something that will strike us as strange when compared to our modern marriage practice, however. There was no dating or trial relationship until you decided to get married. Marriages were arranged. The groom's family had to pay a "bride price" for the bride. In the Oriental weddings of Jesus's day, the groom was the one who acts, and the bride was passive. The wedding ceremony consisted of the groom coming in a procession to pick up his bride and take her to the wedding feast. If the bridegroom did not come and get her, she was not got. In the Old Testament, when God claimed his bride, Israel, Israel was completely passive through all the events of the exodus. They were claimed, delivered from Egypt, and given a new home. In the New Testament, Christ came to our home to claim us, to seek and save the lost. He paid the bride price. Through his cross, he delivered his people from sin and death and will come again to take his bride to his home in heaven and to the wedding feast of the Lamb. It is always God who acts, God who saves, God who delivers, God who claims, God who takes us home. This is why it is called "grace."

But notice that, although we are picked up, we are not picked up like a package. This is not UPS but marriage; not a relationship with an object but a two-way relationship with a living being. Now, it may be true that my body, my mind, my soul, and all those "things" are claimed by him (1 Cor 6:19–20) because he "purchased and won" me, but I am more than those "things." I am a person (Gen 2:7). We are made in his likeness. We have been given significance, endowed with a soul that can love and be loved, make decisions, give, and receive in relationship—at least we could before the fall. Now we are broken shadows of what we were, unable to rightly love God or our neighbor, unable to form perfect relationships. Because I am more than a thing, because I am also a broken person, he must somehow change my heart. He must give me a new heart.

And so, there are two important things to note. First, God has not stopped loving us and wants us back in a right relationship with himself. He took our sin to a cross and paid for our return by his grace. We belong to him because he gave himself for us, and only because he gave himself to us can we give ourselves back to him. We bring nothing to this union but our sin and our need—only after the wedding, after conversion, after faith, do we bring our love and service to him in response. Secondly, our relationship with God is not a relationship of equals, as in human marriage (Gen 1:27). It is a relationship of a Savior to those saved, or better, the relationship of a creator to his creature. "Is not he your father, who created you, who made you and established you?" (Deut 32:6). Father/creator is, of course, another type of family relationship that we have with God. Like marriage, it, too, is a relationship of personal beings, and it, too, is about belonging.

Part 2: Belonging

Creation

In the early church, the doctrine of creation taught a very practical and important fact about our relationship with God. Combes observed that in the early church they believed that all "creation is in bondage, a view of all things being by nature slaves of God in virtue of having been created by him."[7] This was clearly the teaching of the Old Testament, as well as the New. What God made, God owns. Although this worldview lasted into the Middle Ages, it is no longer our way of understanding the world. Now the more common view of the world is the evolution of matter and energy, or at least of a world on its own, operating within its own laws independent of God. And so, modern Christians rarely use creation to establish our identity as those belonging to God. As we have seen, being owned by or responsible to anyone is difficult for modern people, even for Christians. It will be interesting to see what effect modern creationists, interested in scientifically defending the truth of creation, will have on this older idea of also belonging to God.

One of the few modern Christian writers to use the doctrine of creation to define us and our identity was C. S. Lewis. Although Lewis largely stayed out of the evolution/creation debate because he did not consider himself a scientist, he felt that no matter what the mechanics of man's creation, man must be God's creation, and that was the fact that counted.[8] In his book *The Problem of Pain*, Lewis points out that understanding God as our creator is basic to understanding everything about who we are. Being a creature, we are, as he put it, "an essentially dependent being whose principle of existence lies not in itself but in another."[9] However, since human creatures have been given an additional gift of self-awareness, consciousness, and personality, we tend to forget our dependence on God and imagine ourselves as independent beings—with terrible results.

"The existence of a self," writes Lewis, "the mere fact that we call it 'me'—includes, from the first, the danger of self-idolatry." This is, he says, "the 'weak spot' in the very nature of creation, the risk which God apparently thinks worth taking."[10] It is a "weak spot" because God has made himself "capable of being resisted by its own handiwork. . . . This is the most

---

7. Combes, *Metaphor of Slavery*, 125, 161.
8. Lewis, *Problem of Pain*, 72.
9. Lewis, *Problem of Pain*, 75.
10. Lewis, *Problem of Pain*, 81.

astonishing and unimaginable of all the feats we attribute to the Deity."[11] The "self-idolatry" of a dependent being, choosing self over God, then becomes Lewis's definition of sin. The great delusion is when a dependent being "tries to set up on its own, to exist for itself."[12] It may be possible to conclude from Lewis's argument that this danger can be avoided, that it might still be possible for man to resist this self-idolatry and choose not to sin. Adam and Eve may have been able to resist, but we cannot (Gen 5:1–3; Rom 5:12–19). The Bible's teaching of what is usually called original sin makes this impossible. Sinful man is not only ignorant of God but is ignorant of his own ignorance. He is now by nature a deluded and self-idolatrous being.

Lewis certainly speaks as if it were unavoidable. Human beings "desired to be on their own, to take care for their own future, to plan for pleasure and for security, to have a *meum* from which, no doubt, they would pay some reasonable tribute to God in the way of time, attention, and love, but which, nevertheless, was theirs not his. They wanted, as we say, to 'call their souls their own.' But that means to live a lie, for our souls are not, in fact, our own."[13] For Lewis, human independence is an illusion, created by the fact that we can say no to our creator. This is what C. F. Keil once described in his commentary on Genesis as the "imaginary liberty of a sinner."[14] Saying no to our creator, however, is saying no to the source of our existence; it is not freedom—it is death.

I often like to illustrate this point with a story.[15] Once upon a time, there was a disgruntled goldfish who had a nice, large bowl that sat right in the middle of his owner's dining room table. Its bowl was kept very clean, had a few rocks to hide and play in, and he was regularly fed every day. But every day he watched his owner eat his meals, interesting meals with lots of different shapes and colors that the man really seemed to enjoy. All the fish ever got were fish flakes. He watched his owner come and go, sometimes with lots of noise and excitement, going out a door that gave just a glimpse of an interesting and exciting world beyond. All he ever saw were the same rocks in his bowl. He felt like a prisoner. He just had to escape, to

---

11. Lewis, *Problem of Pain*, 127.
12. Lewis, *Problem of Pain*, 75.
13. Lewis, *Problem of Pain*, 80.
14. Kiel and Delitzsch, *Commentary on the Old Testament*, 1:95.
15. There are many versions of this story in modern folklore, from children's stories like *A Fish Out of Water* from Dr. Seuss (published later by his wife, Helen Palmer) to a serious, thought-provoking symbol in *Out of My Mind* by Sharon Draper. It is a common experience with goldfish that lends itself to parables like this one.

get free and enjoy the good life. One day he backed way up into a corner of his bowl, swam with all his might, and shot right out of his bowl. Flying through the air, he yelled, "I'm free!" But, alas, he was not. He hit the floor and in a few moments he was dead.

As Lewis explained, a creature cannot exist apart from its creator. "The place for which he designs them, in his scheme of things, is the place they are made for. When they reach it, their nature is fulfilled and their happiness attained; a broken bone in the universe has been set, the anguish is over. When we want to be something other than the thing God wants us to be, we must be wanting what, in fact, will not make us happy."[16] The creature is, by its very nature, a slave.

Our problem is that we do not know or understand our nature as creatures. We were made to be slaves of God, and our happiness depends on being slaves of God, but we will have nothing of it. "Now God, who has made us, knows what we are and that our happiness lies in him," writes Lewis, "yet we will not seek it in him as long as he leaves us any other resort where it can even plausibly be looked for. While what we call 'our own life' remains agreeable we will not surrender it to him. What then can God do in our interest but make 'our own life' less agreeable to us and take away the plausible sources of false happiness? . . . The creature's illusion of self-sufficiency must, for the creature's sake, be shattered."[17] Hence the reason God allows suffering and pain in our lives—to teach us our need for him, to recenter our lives and hope in him alone.

This is not Schleiermacher's famous definition of faith as a "feeling of dependence on God." It is not a feeling, nor a psychological experience, nor a choice, but a cold hard fact of our existence. Creatures belong to their maker. We are what he makes us, not what we imagine or would like ourselves to be. Because of our fallen nature, we reject this and have cut ourselves off from him and from the only source of life. We cannot fix this by recognizing our creatureliness and putting ourselves back in a right relationship with God. That ship has sailed. We are the broken children of Adam and Eve, already imperfect and sinful. This broken relationship is mended only when we find our true master in Christ, who died to win our forgiveness and give us back our real lives. This is a return to the reality we were made for. Besides, what he makes us in Christ is far better than

---

16. Lewis, *Problem of Pain*, 52.
17. Lewis, *Problem of Pain*, 96–97.

anything we could make of ourselves or even imagine (1 Cor 2:9), far better than life in a fishbowl!

Kingdom

And this brings us to our third defining relationship in what it means to belong to God—a king and his subjects. This is not strictly a family relationship, though kings were often referred to as the "fathers" of their subjects. Fathers, especially in our culture, may not be seen as authority figures, but there can be no mistake about a king. This is a relationship about authority. It follows naturally from the idea of creator as owner and ruler of all he has made.

Many Jewish prayers begin with "Blessed are you, Lord our God, king of everything." The authority of an earthly king, however, is not that of the creator; it is delegated authority. The fourth commandment, about the authority of parents and all governing authorities, follows the first three commandments about the authority of God because human authorities are delegated authorities. Like slaves, all we ever have is delegated authority, representing our master. Whether governmental authority is understood as delegated by God directly, as in the "divine right of kings," or through the people, as in democratic theory, or by default, as in the law of the jungle (evolution), it has been a source of much disagreement among political philosophers. All these ideas could also be found in the first century, as in our own time. Some say it makes no difference which it is just so long as some authority is keeping order in the world. But of course, it makes a great difference. It turns out to be quite an important thing for us when we say that Christ is our lord or our king. That statement cost many early Christians their lives.

Since kings and kingdoms are not as familiar to us today, especially ancient Oriental kings, the concept may need a little explanation. Most kings in the ancient world claimed the favor of their gods, but in the ancient Middle East, there was an important difference. These kings claimed to actually be gods. Pharaoh was a god and so were the kings of Mesopotamia and China. Sometimes the king was understood to be an incarnation of a god or perhaps the offspring of a god who mated with a mortal, but either way, once you are dealing with a god, power becomes absolute. The king's voice was the voice of a god and so must be obeyed or terrible things would result. Since the gods created them, the people belonged to their god-king, who could do with them as he wished, granting life or death at will. Since the gods created the earth, all the land of the kingdom belonged to the king to do with as he wished. He could take any property as his own, though to ensure their loyalty, he allowed his nobles to use it as their own. All the subjects of an Oriental king were quite literally his slaves.

The root of the Hebrew word for king, *melek*, is found in almost all Semitic languages. It comes from a root word meaning "to possess" or "own exclusively," and a parallel Assyrian word, *malaku*, meaning "to have the final word," "to command."[18] It is like another Semitic word, *ba'al*, which as a verb means "to possess" or "own," but as a noun means "master" or "lord."[19] This is why *ba'al*, you may remember, is used in the Old Testament as a general word for a false god. Whether *melek* or *ba'al*, such words describe someone who owns you and can tell you what to do. This is the Eastern idea of the king. He is a god, and his subjects are his slaves.

On the upside, there can be no doubt that the benefits of centralized power and organization helped to create great civilizations, but there was also a downside. The gods were fickle, capricious, vengeful, selfish, greedy, and arrogant, and so were many of these kings who claimed to be gods. Greek civilization especially grew to hate the very idea of having a king and being subject to the arbitrary whims of a man often ruled by his passions. This was, to them, the definition of chaos! They prized being levelheaded, reasonable, fair, and just. The mind was to rule the passions. Why couldn't people be ruled by a system of reasonable laws (a constitution) established by those who had to live under them? Very early in their history, the Greeks, and later the Romans, got rid of their kings. They were replaced by the rule of law. Instead of belonging to a king or a kingdom, a Greek felt that he belonged to his city, a *polis*, a constitutional entity governed by an assembly of citizens under its rules. He was expected to give his fortune and his life to his city if required. He obeyed its laws as the obligation or "social contract" under which they lived.

Tom Holland suggests that the concept of democracy developed from the Greek way of fighting as a unit, where each citizen depended on the shield of the citizen standing next to him, creating a sense of equality, interdependence, and cooperation that led eventually to the idea of shared political power.[20] Whether or not this is true, non-Greeks, slaves, women,

18. Brown et al., *New Brown, Driver and Briggs*, 572.
19. Brown et al., *New Brown, Driver and Briggs*, 127.
20. Holland, *Persian Fire*, xv–xvii, 99–142. See esp. 138.

What Does It Mean to Belong?

and the poor were excluded from any share in this democracy. To a Greek citizen of a *polis*, freedom meant that no human being had a natural right to tell him what to do. The Greeks even elected their generals by ballot. Some Greeks kept their kings, like the Spartans, who had two of them at the same time as checks on each other, and whose power was further limited by law and custom. To the Greeks, all Asians who were ruled by god-kings were nothing but contemptible slaves, while they alone were free.

Romans, like the Greeks before them, banished their kings and established a constitutional republic. Rome was a *polis* but a *polis* that ended up ruling the world; there were no nations or countries in our sense of the word. Eventually civil wars destroyed the republic, and Rome was then ruled by a dictator. But throughout their entire history, a Roman dictator dared never use the title of "king."[21] Julius Caesar was assassinated because he was seen to be making himself a king. This dictator called himself *princeps* (first citizen) and ran his laws through the senate to rubber-stamp them. After Rome conquered the Asiatic kingdoms of the East, however, things changed. The people there, who had a long history of thinking in terms of god-kings, built temples for the worship of the Caesars. It wasn't long before the emperors began to build temples for themselves in Rome too. The first emperor, Augustus, added "son of god" to his many titles while Caligula, thirty years later, demanded to be worshiped as one. Later emperors were worshiped only after their death. Vespasian was making a bad joke when he quipped on his death bed, "Oh dear, I think I'm becoming a god."[22]

It wasn't only the Greeks and Romans who had problems with kings, however. Israel did as well, or, we should say, the God of Israel did as well. In Egypt, Jacob's family grew from a family into very large tribal clans. But since they were slaves, they had no real governing system. When Moses brought them out of Egypt, they were given a governing structure, a whole set of civic laws from God. Moses, however, was still the sole leader of the people. But he was not a king. He combined the positions of prophet (messenger of God), priest (he was a Levite who set up the worship system), and judge (governor).

"Judge" was the sixteenth-century word used in the King James Version for the Hebrew *shepheteem*, which means "the one who makes judgments, decides, or governs." Modern readers expect a judge to be a person

---

21. Beard, *SPQR*, 355–56.
22. Beard, *SPQR*, 428–32.

who sits in a court room and so are often confused by this title. A *shepheteem* could judge as in a legal case, but in the book of Judges, it would be better translated as "leader," "governor" or even "champion" since they usually led God's people to military victories. The translators of the King James Version saw them as bringing God's judgment on the enemies of Israel and so called them judges.

These judges were not elected or born into this position, nor did they take it for themselves. They were ordinary people called by God for a special task, usually to rescue God's people from their enemies. Once the task was done, they reverted to being just another Israelite. When Gideon was done with his task as judge, the people wanted to make him a king, but he refused, saying, "I will not rule over you . . . the LORD will rule over you" (Judg 8:22–23). And here was the problem. In the East, kings were thought of as gods, and Israel had only one God.

In the time of Samuel, who, like Moses, was another example of a prophet/priest/judge, the people complained because they did not like the system of waiting for God to raise up someone to rescue them from their enemies. They wanted a king like the other nations because then they would have a system already in place to face emergencies, like a standing army. God tells Samuel, "They have not rejected you, but they have rejected me from being king over them. . . . Obey their voice; only you shall solemnly warn them and show them the ways of the king who shall reign over them" (1 Sam 8:7–9). Samuel warns them about what a king will take from them, but they are not dissuaded. God grants them a king, but he cannot be like the typical Eastern king; he cannot be a god-king. God alone owns the people, and he alone tells them what to do (Exod 19:3–6). If Israel will have a king, he is to be God's servant and under his authority. So, God lays down some ground rules: "If you will fear the LORD and serve him and obey his voice and not rebel against the commandment of the LORD, and if both you and the king who reigns over you will follow the LORD your God, it will be well. But if you will not obey the voice of the LORD, but rebel against the commandment of the LORD, then the hand of the LORD will be against you and your king" (1 Sam 12:14–15).

Israel must never forget that it has but one God and the king is to be a servant-king responsible to him for the care of his people. The king is not an absolute monarch. This may be the first historical example of the separation of church and state, or better, a separation of powers, administrative and priestly functions (1 Sam 13:8–14), though both are to submit to God's word. All other ancient states combined church and state, usually in the person of the king.[23] This new concept would have a profound effect on the Christian West, not only in the case of limiting the power of kings and protecting the rights of their subjects under God, but it would also affect our understanding of political leaders as servants responsible to a higher authority. Remember that in Luther's understanding of the two kingdoms, political leaders are also servants of God (Rom 13:4) and are responsible for taking care of his creation. Today, however, we call our elected leaders "servants of the people." Still, everyone knows that they are often slaves to their own ambition and to powerful people they wish to please and not solely interested in what is best for the people. Medieval kings at least pretended that they were servants of God (and sometimes they actually were).

Israel, however, is a theocracy with a servant-king explicitly tasked with carrying out the will of God as God has revealed it. Israel's kings are not elected. God will choose them from among the people, and their sons may be allowed to rule after them if they remain faithful to God. The king is always one among equals. He is, in many ways, in the position of a "permanent judge." God then chooses the line of David to reign "forever," but most of his descendants are a disappointment. So, God ends the line of kings from the house of David, but he does not end the line of David (2 Sam 7). It looks like the tree of David has been cut down but "a shoot will come up from the stump of Jesse" (Isa 11:1 NIV).

The promise of a coming king from David's line is fulfilled in Jesus, a descendant of David, but whose only earthly crown is of thorns. He is the ultimate servant-king, one among equals (Deut 18:15–19), fully human, standing with sinners in our great need. Jesus is the last and greatest prophet, priest, and judge/king, sent to rescue us from our enemies of sin, death, and the devil. But he is also what all the other Oriental kings were not: God in the flesh—a real God-king. When Jesus stood before Pilate, he confessed that he was a king (John 18:36–37, see also 1 Tim 6:13–16) but that he would not use his power in a way that a Roman, a Greek, an Egyptian, or a Persian would understand. Jesus said, "Everyone who is of the truth listens to my voice" (John 18:37). He did not mean simply to hear but to heed, to hear and obey, to follow. Christ's kingdom is made up of those who put their faith in Jesus and are obedient to him.

23. Church and state can also be combined in democracies and other states. Remember the state executed Socrates for impiety and corrupting the religion of the youth. In Rome, Christians were executed for not offering a sacrifice to Caesar. Even in our day, "statism" has come to mean much more than simple economic control by the state.

When Jesus describes his followers as "everyone who is of the truth," the Greek word for truth is no doubt used in the Hebrew sense. *Emeth* not only means "factually true," "accurate," and "real," but also "to *be* true," i.e., "faithful," "obedient." We are of the truth because we are obedient and faithful. "My sheep hear my voice, and I know them, and they follow me. I give them eternal life, and they will never perish, and no one will snatch them out of my hand. My Father, who has given them to me, is greater than all, and no one is able to snatch them out of the Father's hand. I and the Father are one" (John 10:27–30). To be "in his hand" describes another aspect of belonging to the ruler of life and death.

If I put myself "in your hands," I am in your power. You may do with me as you want. I recognize that you have the power to ignore me, abuse me, throw me away, or help me. "Putting myself into your hands" implies I am trusting you to help me, rescue me, and do what is best for me. All creatures must recognize that they are under the power of their creator God. He may do with us whatever he wishes, but we trust him to help, rescue, and do what is best for us—not because we deserve this but only for the sake of his mercy in Jesus. Only with confidence in Jesus can we pray at the hour of our death what Jesus prayed in the hour of his: "Father, into your hands I commit my spirit" (Luke 23:46; Ps 31:5). We belong to him, and not even death can snatch us out of this hand.

Jesus was the last great descendant of David (Rom 1:3), coming to fulfill Israel's purpose of winning the blessing of forgiveness for all nations (Gen 12:3). The new Israel, the people belonging to God through faith in Christ Jesus (Gal 6:16; Rom 2:28–29; 4:16–17; 11:26; 1 Pet 1:1), is once more ruled directly by God—not in a state or by any earthly form of government. Jesus rules as absolute king from within our hearts as we follow his word (Luke 17:20–21). The kingdom of God exists wherever there are people who listen to him. We confess in the creed one holy Christian and apostolic church based on the witness/writings of the apostles (John 17:20). No matter which country we live in, this one church serves king Jesus. As his subjects, we support and serve our earthly governments (Rom 13:1–7) in everything not contrary to the will of God, assisting in its God-given mandate to administer justice, punish evil, and provide law and order. We must pray for "kings and all those in authority" so that Christians may be free to live their faith and share it with others (1 Tim 2:1–4). But our first and greatest loyalty is always to Jesus.

What Does It Mean to Belong?

Subject or a Citizen?

Jesus is an absolute monarch. We may be subject to the authority and power of others, but we are to be obedient to Jesus over all these. We are subjects of his kingdom, and yet St. Paul famously refers to us not as subjects but as citizens; he calls us "citizens of heaven" (Phil 3:20) and "fellow citizens with the saints" (Eph 2:19). What did Paul mean when he borrowed that word from the Greco-Roman world, a world without kings, and does it suggest a different way of understanding God's authority over us? Do we have a say, a vote, a share in deciding the way things are to go?

The fundamental difference between a subject and a citizen was nicely described in 1789, right after the American Revolutionary War, in a popular pamphlet on the subject that circulated in the former colonies: "A subject is one who is under the power of another, but a citizen is an unit of a mass of free people, who, collectively, possess sovereignty."[24] And there it is. The issue is sovereignty, power. Who is in control? Where does the authority lie? Who has the right to tell us who we are or what we can do? Is it man or God? The word "citizenship" comes from a system where the right to rule belongs to the people. Theoretically, citizens have more power and control over decisions of government than a subject. When the Greeks and the Romans got rid of their kings, they changed their system of authority; they did not get rid of it. Instead of rule by one person, a king, they substituted rule either by people voting for those who rule (a republic) or voting directly for their laws (democracy), an expression of what was called in 1789 "collective sovereignty" or rule by the people. Those who governed were expected to govern according to the rules of either a written constitution or other system of laws and customs made by the people that limited their power (Rome did not have a written constitution, and neither does the United Kingdom today). No ruler was to be above the law.

The real issue, however, may not be one of who has the power but the issue of whether individual freedom to do as we like is protected and not interfered with. A king can protect an individual's freedoms or take them away and so can a democracy or a republic. A citizen has rights and responsibilities, and a subject has privileges and responsibilities. They may turn out to be much the same thing in the end. If you are treated well, if your freedoms are protected, any government system will do. This, at least, seems to be the lesson of history.

---

24. Ramsay, "Dissertation," para. 1.

Part 2: Belonging

Citizenship in ancient Rome did not include any input or say in government. In the late Empire voting disappeared completely. In her history of Rome, Mary Beard reminds us: "The Romans did not fight for 'democracy'; they fought for 'freedom.'"[25] Citizenship to a Roman (and I think to most people today) meant the protection of their freedoms—freedom to go where you want and do what you want (within the law); freedom from arrest, punishment, and seizure of property without due process or trial; freedom to make legally binding contracts (including wills, marriages, etc.); freedom of speech and access to information; and freedom from being enslaved and other forms of exploitation.[26] Because the emperor protected these rights, the Romans considered themselves a free people even though they lived in a dictatorship.

Most people will accept some external controls on their behavior (government, parents, teachers, law enforcement, etc.) as long as the answer to the question "Who decides what is best for me?" can be answered with "I do." The best form of government is the one that allows us the most freedom to do what we want. The most reliable protection for private freedoms may be provided in a political system such as democracy, where citizens have some control, but the issue of sovereignty, of control, still remains. Although democracy may be an excellent political system, it is an impossible system in our relationship with God.

Paul said, "Indeed there are many 'gods' and many 'lords'—yet for us there is one God, the Father, from whom are all things and for whom we exist, and one Lord, Jesus Christ, for whom are all things and through whom we exist" (1 Cor 8:5–6). For the Christian, there is only one sovereign, one authority, and he is to have our allegiance and obedience in all things in life. He is in control. We are his subjects and not free citizens who can go our own way. Remember, though, that going our own way is not the definition of freedom. It is a mirage—it looks like water but is only more sand. If it is not God's way, it is the wrong way, the way of pain, suffering, and death. "All we like sheep have gone astray; we have turned—everyone—to his own way; and the Lord has laid on him the iniquity of us all" (Isa 53:6). Real freedom is to be God's forgiven child, free of sin, death, and hell.

So what are we to make of Paul's use of the word "citizen?" Paul calls us "citizens of heaven" in Phil 3:18–20: "Many . . . walk as enemies of the cross of Christ. Their end is destruction, their god is the belly, and they

---

25. Beard, *SPQR*, 189.
26. Beard, *SPQR*, 189.

glory in their shame, with minds set on earthly things. But our citizenship is in heaven, and from it we await a Savior, the Lord Jesus Christ." Many commentaries on this verse suggest that because Philippi was a Roman colony, they would understand Paul to be talking about "dual citizenship," being citizens of two places at the same time. Even Paul, you remember, had dual citizenship, being a citizen of both Tarsus and Rome. Is Paul saying that we have dual citizenship on earth and in heaven at the same time? Does this mean that "when in Rome" we can "do as the Romans do"—that here on earth we are in control?

Beard, in her history of Rome, claims that to be a citizen of two places at once was an invention of Rome, and she makes the development of the idea of Roman citizenship for everyone in the Empire a main theme of her book.[27] Dual citizenship, however, existed in the Greek world (called *isopoliteia*) for three centuries before it did in Rome.[28] Even so, Paul is not referring to dual citizenship in this passage. Sherwin-White explains:

> *Politeumata* [citizenship] is not *polis* or *politeia*: it is community not citizenship. . . . The metaphor is in terms of the city-state but not wider. Paul is contrasting Christians with the men of this world. Technically the term *politeumata* was used in connexion with the great cities . . . to denote self-sufficient and self-governing communities of noncitizens, especially of Jews, who form a city within a city . . . who were under the general authority of the citizen body but organized their own internal affairs. The Jewish synagogues and Sanhedrins were such *politeumata* in some cities. The metaphor would come naturally to the mind of a travelled Jew, who had seen the Jewish *politeumata* of half Asia. The point of the metaphor in Philippians is that the Christians are not citizens but resident aliens in the cities of the world, and they follow their own rules.[29]

Paul is not saying you can "do as the Romans do"—that different rules apply in different places. Christians are "resident aliens," subjects of a foreign power, living as "resident aliens in the cities of the world" (see 1 Pet 2:11–12). As such, we live by the rules of our king and not by the rules of where we are living at the moment (Matt 15:9). Where these rules agree or at least do not conflict with our king, we can live together with the

---

27. Beard, *SPQR*, 166.
28. Sherwin-White, *Roman Society and Roman Law*, 178.
29. Sherwin-White, *Roman Society and Roman Law*, 185.

world cooperatively and peacefully. But we should know where the lines are and stay on our side. *The Theological Dictionary of the New Testament* warns us about words like "citizenship": "The words 'politea' [citizen] and 'politeusthi' [citizenship] lose their flavour at the point where Hellenism and Judaism meet. This is because the society to which the Jew belongs, in consequence of the totalitarian religious claim, bears a different character from that of the society in which these words have their true home."[30] "Totalitarian religious claim" refers to their belief that God is their master, and they are his slaves.

And so, the rule is that the meaning of a borrowed word like "citizenship" should be determined by its use in the adopting culture, not by the dictionary. This works both ways, of course. It is also true when Hebrew words are taken over into a Greek context. For example, it was in Antioch, a Greek city, that the disciples were first called Christians (Acts 11:26). "Christ" is the title given Jesus, the literal translation of the Hebrew word Messiah, meaning "anointed one." In the Greek context, however, this word had no meaning. They did not anoint their kings or their priests or their prophets. They did not know the Old Testament context where the word referred to the coming of an "anointed one" from the line of David who would suffer and save us from our sins. To them it was just part of a compound name, and a strange name at that.

Why would you call someone "anointed?" They heard it, instead, as "Chrestos," a very common name for slaves (meaning "useful"). But if Chrestos was the lord of these people, then the people of Antioch meant to say, and grammatically did say, that these people belonged to Christ. F. F. Bruce explains that the word "Christian" "is formed from the title Christos by the addition of the colloquial suffix *-ianos* (the naturalized Greek form of the Latin suffix *-ianus*). The suffix was used among other things to denote a man's slaves and other members of his household."[31] To the Greeks, "Christian" meant a slave of Christ. They were more right than they knew.

---

30. Strahmann, *Theological Dictionary*, 6:526.

31. Bruce, *New Testament History*, 297. He also notes here that the Roman historian, Suetonius, reported that Claudius expelled the Jews from Rome because of riots among the Jews over some person called Chrestus. Bruce takes this to be disagreements among the Jews over Christ when Christianity first came to Rome: "Christus, not unnaturally confused with the common slave name Chrestus, which was pronounced in practically the same way."

What Does It Mean to Belong?

The word *politase* or citizen is only used four times in the New Testament and never in the Greek sense of belonging to a self-governing, decision-making political body. In Heb 8:11 it is usually translated as "neighbor" from the sense of living closely together as you do in a city. When the prodigal son has spent all his money, he attaches himself to a citizen of that country (Luke 15:15), again, meaning simply a "resident." In the parable of the ten minas (Luke 19:12), the citizens who want their king removed are called *politie*—not *douloi* (slaves) like those who receive the minas from their king. Once more, this means only that they were "economically and personally 'independent inhabitants.'"[32] In fact, this turns out to be a problem. They want independent political power and to be free of their king, and they are punished severely for it. Here is an ominous warning about wanting the independence of a citizen from our rightful king, Jesus.

The other use of the word also has nothing to do with political power or citizenship. In Acts 21:39 Paul says that he is a citizen of Tarsus while elsewhere he is simply said to be a Roman. None of these uses are in reference to citizenship per se but only to the legal protections and treatment of a Roman citizen.[33] In Eph 2:12, non-Jews were "separated from Christ, alienated from the commonwealth [*politea*] of Israel and strangers to the covenants of promise, having no hope and without God." And then a few verses later, in Eph 2:19, after coming to faith in Christ, they are said to be "no longer strangers and aliens, but you are fellow citizens [*sympolitoi*] with the saints and members of the household of God." As with Paul and Rome, they share the privileges and benefits of belonging to the family of God and will be treated like family. They do not become citizens of the state of Israel but members of the family. The ancient family structure was not democratic, as we shall see. The point of the comparison is only that we belong to the family of God not like a Greek or a Roman belonged to their city.

---

32. Strathmann, *Theological Dictionary*, 6:534.
33. Strathmann, *Theological Dictionary*, 6:543.

CHAPTER 5

Born a Slave

"Jesus answered, 'Truly, truly, I say to you, unless one is born of water and the Spirit, he cannot enter the kingdom of God.'"—JOHN 3:5

IN THE ANCIENT WORLD there were four ways that people became slaves. From the most likely to the least likely, they were:

1. Capture. Most slaves were captured in battle (or stolen/kidnapped). Capture and then the subsequent sale and purchase produced the greatest number of slaves.

2. Birth. The next greatest source of slaves came from being born to a slave, or if you were abandoned at birth and left to die, someone could take you and raise you as a slave.[1]

3. Purchase. As an existing slave you could be sold at any time, or if you were a child, your family could sell you if they were poor or to pay a debt. A court could order you to be sold to pay your debt (Matt 18:25).

4. Self-sale. Roman law allowed you to sell yourself into slavery as a last resort to survive if you were starving or in the hope of improving your position if you could work for a wealthy and powerful master who would later reward you with freedom. In fact, although the ancients said it was done, there is very little evidence of actual historical cases.[2]

---

1. We might misunderstand phrases like "I am your servant, the son of your handmaid" (Ps 86:16). Here *Eved* means slave and *Amath* means slave woman: "I was born a slave in your house and belong to your family." This could express pride, or a sense of my obligation to you and your obligation to me. Interesting when said to God.

2. Byron, *Recent Research*, 142; Crook, *Law and Life of Rome*, 59–60. The most

Since slavery was so abhorrent and the likelihood of abuse so high, this would have been very rare.

Christians become the slaves of Christ in all these ways, except perhaps the last. Jesus our king fought for us and gave his life to pay for our sin, thus both "winning us" as spoils of war (Phil 3:12; 2 Cor 2:14; Rom 11:7; Eph 3:1) and at the same time "purchasing" us with his blood (Rev 5:9; 2 Pet 2:11; 1 Cor 6:20; 7:23; Acts 20:28; Exod 6:4; Ps 74:2). All Christians are especially said to be "born of God" (John 1:12–13; 3:3). But there is the same problem with self-sale to God as there was with self-sale into slavery in the ancient world. Since we are spiritually dead sinners and unwilling and unable to give ourselves to God (Rom 8:7; 1 Cor 2:14; Eph 2:8–9), the natural man would consider slavery to God abhorrent and an abuse of his freedom. So, we would not expect to see the concept of self-sale to God in the Scriptures. Responding to God's call, which he enables us both to will and to do (Phil 2:13), is everywhere in the Bible, but not people making a calculated decision to belong to God (John 1:12–13; see also Matt 19:21–26). To better understand this difference, let's back up and consider how we can be born of God, born a slave, or better, reborn a slave of Christ.

Baptism

In his book on slavery in the New Testament, Harris writes, "Baptism is the rite that marks a transfer of ownership."[3] He cites Matt 28:19, "baptizing them into the name," and notes that the Greek says "into" (*eis*) and not "in" (*ev*). "'Into the name of,'" he states, is the usual Greek way of denoting a change of ownership. This is why Paul is careful in 1 Cor 1:12–15 to say that no one was baptized "into" his name or anyone else's name, as if they now belonged to someone other than Christ. In baptism "the person baptized passes into the possession of the Triune God."[4] With the water, the name of God—Father, Son, and Holy Spirit—is put on the forehead of those baptized. God signs his name on his property, at the same time signing his promise to forgive us and claim us as his own for Jesus's sake whenever we

---

common examples were plain fraud, where someone is sold by an accomplice pretending to be a slave and then proves their free *status* so they can walk away with the money. There are also cases of "contract" servitude, or indentured servitude, but this was not intended to be permanent, even if it did sometimes turn out that way.

3. Harris, *Slave of Christ*, 109–10.
4. Harris, *Slave of Christ*, 110.

seek his forgiveness. In this way, we are able to *use* our baptism throughout life as an assurance whenever we repent of sin. If baptism makes us God's possession, it can only do so by giving us faith in this promise. This was the understanding not only of Scripture but also of the early church.

When J. G. Davies discusses the church fathers of the early second century (Ignatius, Justin Martyr, Irenaeus, etc.) and their views on baptism, he writes:

> The second-century Fathers believed that baptism was a means of conveying the Holy Spirit; it provided weapons for spiritual combat; it mediated the remission of sins and illumination; it initiated into the Chosen People and was therefore "spiritual circumcision" in contradistinction to the carnal circumcision of the Old Israel; it was a means of rebirth, and was the "seal" of eternal life. This final term "seal" was applied frequently to baptism during this period. The word was used of a mark to identify property, and owners branded their livestock with such a mark. Since therefore to be initiated is to be stamped with the indelible mark of the name of Christ, the candidates thereby becoming God's property, baptism was known as the "seal."[5]

Harris begins well with his understanding of baptism as a "transfer of ownership," but since he does not understand baptism as giving the faith that makes us God's own possession, he must then see dedication to God as a separate transaction after coming to faith. "Through baptism they have become eternally bound to him by mutual agreement."[6] Baptism is how someone who first comes to faith will then "indicate that they love their new master and pledge to serve him wholeheartedly as long as they live."[7] Thus baptism becomes a way to "sell yourself" into slavery to Christ. First you come to faith and then use baptism as your act of dedication to him to receive his mark of ownership—but these two cannot be separated. When you come to faith, you are his possession. Whether you come to faith by baptism or by the word, it is faith that makes us his possession. And neither one is our doing. He reasons, as many do, that since God does "not force us against our will," we must "voluntarily embrace slavery" to Christ.[8] But this is faulty logic. When talking about becoming a Christian, "forced" and

---

5. Davies, *Early Christian Church*, 104.
6. Harris, *Slave of Christ*, 110.
7. Harris, *Slave of Christ*, 110.
8. Harris, *Slave of Christ*, 115.

"voluntary" are not opposites. Just because conversion is not forced does not mean that it must be voluntary.

Birth

The best way to understand this is to look at it the way the Bible does, as a new or second birth (John 3:5; Titus 3:5–6). One does not choose, demand, ask, or deserve to be born; one is given birth. It is a gift. It makes no sense to say either that I chose to be born or that I was given life against my will—I had no will before I existed. It makes no logical sense to say the gift of life was "forced" on me if I am free to refuse it at any time, kill myself, and throw it away. On the one hand, I have no power to choose it; I cannot give myself life. I cannot make my heart to beat or my lungs to breathe. On the other hand, once life is given, I have the choice to care for it (feed, protect, exercise it) or throw it away (kill it). Faith works in much the same way.

The Bible teaches that baptism is not a tool man uses to make an "agreement" with God but a tool God uses to give us life, life with him, through trust in his Son. Let me list just a few of the passages: "He came to his own, and his own people did not receive him. But to all who did receive him, who believed in his name, he gave the right to become children of God, who were born, not of blood nor of the will of the flesh nor of the will of man, but of God" (John 1:11–13). "You have been born again, not of perishable seed, but of imperishable, through the living and enduring word of God" (1 Pet 1:23 NIV). "The words that I have spoken to you are spirit and life" (John 6:63). "Jesus answered him, 'Truly, truly, I say to you, unless one is born again [the Greek *anothen* can also mean "from above"] he cannot see the kingdom of God. . . . Unless one is born of water and the Spirit, he cannot enter the kingdom of God. That which is born of the flesh is flesh, and that which is born of the Spirit is spirit" (John 3:3–6). "He saved us, not because of righteous things we had done, but because of his mercy. He saved us through the washing of rebirth and renewal by the Holy spirit, whom he poured out on us generously through Jesus Christ our Savior, so that, having been justified by his grace, we might become heirs having the hope of eternal life" (Titus 3:5–7 NIV). "Repent and be baptized every one of you in the name of Jesus Christ for the forgiveness of your sins, and you will receive the gift of the Holy Spirit. For the promise is for you and for your children" (Acts 2:38–39). "Go therefore and make disciples of all nations, baptizing them in the name of the Father and of the Son and of the Holy Spirit, teaching them to observe all that I have commanded you" (Matt 28:19–20).

As in childbirth where the gift of life is simply given, so in the birth of faith, trust in Jesus (spiritual life) is simply given, implanted by the Spirit of God working through word (or word and water, as in baptism) so that we believe the promise of forgiveness and eternal life in Jesus. Our only choice, once it is given, is to feed it with God's word and sacrament; to protect it against our sinful nature, the world, and the devil; and to exercise it in love for our neighbor—or to reject it. The more we understand life as gift, whether physical life or spiritual, the more impossible it becomes for us to understand why anyone would want to throw it away. The "death wish" is a mystery both to psychology and to theology, although we know it is a real part of our broken human nature. The comparison of faith to a birth may help explain why God gets all the credit for our conversion and we get all the blame for rejecting it. Even so, this will always remain a paradox to our limited understanding.

The birth of faith is not the result of either free will or of force any more than physical birth is. Faith is that miracle of God working through his word to take an unwilling heart and make it a willing heart. We have free will in many things, but when it comes to trust and love for God, we are powerless (1 Cor 2:12–14). Harris does raise the question, "Is slavery to Christ in any sense self-imposed?" And to answer this question, he compares 1 Cor 6:20, "you were bought" (God's act), with 1 Thess 1:9, "you turned to God" (a human act), observing that, somehow, they both must be true.[9] As for how they can both be true, he simply says, "Never forget the provenience of God's grace with respect to all human virtue."[10] God is somehow either the cause, or contributes in some way, to man's response to God, and he leaves it at that.[11] However, we must not leave it at that.

Man has no power to choose God any more than a dead man can choose to live (Eph 2:1–5; 1 Cor 1:27–31; 2:14). Faith is the change of a dead heart, a "heart of stone," as Ezekiel says (Ezek 36:26), into a living one—an unwilling heart into a willing heart. When Paul says in 1 Thess 1:9, "You turned to God," it is perfectly true, they did, but it was a willing heart

---

9. Harris, *Slave of Christ*, 115.

10. Harris, *Slave of Christ*, 115.

11. Harris, *Slave of Christ*, 115. Though he is not clear on how the will of man is involved, he does conclude here by citing Rev 5:9 that "Christ bought us. We did not sell ourselves to him." Although he agrees that selling yourself has no parallel in the Christian life, he does not deal with the implications.

given by God that moved them. This is why psychologically, when an adult comes to faith it "feels" like a decision, while to someone baptized as an infant and raised (fed) on God's word it "feels" like they have always had faith. The reality, however, is in both cases caused by a heart changed by God. In Ps 22:9, David says that God is both the cause of his birth and the cause of his faith: "You are he who took me from the womb; you made me trust you at my mother's breasts." The verbs are causative: "the one who caused my breaking forth from the womb" also "caused me to trust in you." God is the cause of both physical birth and the birth of faith.

Baptism is indeed "the rite that marks the transfer of ownership," but it is not like a contract; it is like a birth (rebirth) into a new family—one we did not choose but one which claims us. We are born by the Spirit—graciously chosen (John 15:16), summoned ("called"), adopted, and welcomed by God. God created us without our aid; God redeemed us without our aid; God brought us to faith without our aid; and at death he will take us to his home without our aid. Salvation is by grace alone. Grace is an all-or-nothing word. A gift is not a gift if I must "chip in" on it. A living faith does not make "mutual agreements" with God; rather, God does it all. He dies for us; he opens our eyes; he turns on the light; we see God's claim on us; we respond in love and obedience. We are "his workmanship, created in Christ Jesus" (Eph 2:10).

While talking about birth as a way of belonging to the family of God, we should note the word "adopted" I used above. Paul also uses this Roman practice to describe a relationship of belonging to God. It has often been said the Romans did not have children—they took children. If you were a Roman, simply having a child did not make it yours, not unless the father took the child as his own. Otherwise, the child was killed or exposed—taken out and left somewhere to die. The *pater familia* decided if a child born to him would live or die. It was his choice to take it or leave it. In the same way, Roman law allowed him to take or adopt someone else's child (or adult) as a son and heir even if this person was not born to him. Famously, Julius Caesar had a biological son but adopted Octavian (Augustus) as his son and heir. Paul said that sinners outside the family of God are chosen by him for Jesus's sake to become his children (John 15:16). We are "adopted" back into the family of God when we no longer belonged to it because of sin (Rom 8:15, 23). In this sense, of course, even the baptized are adopted back into the family of God.

Part 2: Belonging

It is worth saying again, however, that there is more than one means of grace, more than one way in which God can create or deliver faith and make us children of God. Paul says in Rom 10:17 "faith comes from hearing the message" (NIV). It is the message, deliverd by word and water, the proclamation of the good news declaring us forgiven, that draws us to believe and trust that promise (John 6:44). Like the *pater familia*, he declares it, and we are his. God makes Christians in both ways, through baptism and through hearing the declaration of the gospel promise. Although those who come to faith through hearing the message will then be baptized (Mark 16:16), this is not a separate transaction with God. Faith makes us God's possession whether it comes by baptism or by hearing. Those baptized after coming to faith receive the Holy Spirit (Acts 2:38–39), only in their case not to create faith but to strengthen and confirm it.

In the Roman world a slave could not be adopted without first being freed. In other words, you could not legally be a slave and an adopted child at the same time. However, as we noted before, a slave can be treated like a son, even given the rights of a son, and a son can be treated like a slave with the same expectation of obedience. On the other hand, if both the child and the slave are given the same promise, if they are treated the same, with the same love and grace, and are given the same rights, privileges, and obligations, then the distinction between child and slave essentially disappears. As we said at the beginning of this section, everything depends on how your master chooses to treat you.

CHAPTER 6

The Marks of Belonging

IF YOU SAW A crowd of people in the ancient forum at Rome, you would not be able to tell the slaves from the free. A slave would look just the same as everyone else, with perhaps plainer clothes and very short hair.[1] Plain clothes cost less, and short hair helped to keep the slave clean and free of lice. A female slave's hair, of course, was also sold for wigs and hair pieces. A slave's dress and hair style depended, as did everything else, on the whims of a master who often did not want to spend much on the upkeep of a slave. When a slave was freed, both men and women would grow their hair long as a way of showing their new *status*. Christians, however, were urged to dress simply (1 Pet 3:3), and the men were urged to cut their hair short to avoid vanity (1 Cor 11:14; see also Apostolic Constitutions 1.3).[2] That Christians would have had plain clothes and short hair would have made them look very much like slaves. Perhaps that was not an accident. Many of them were slaves, and the others were meant to be examples of humility.

We should always remember that skin color and other ethnic features meant little in that society and would not have been used to set slaves apart. Slaves could be from any ethnic group from anywhere in the world. But the flip side of this ethnic blindness was also true. Romans were not just from Rome, or even from Italy. Rome was an open society. "Romans could come from anywhere, any level, low born or slave."[3] Emperors and senators could come from Spain, Gaul, North Africa, or any province. The emperor who succeeded Commodus, for example, was even the son of a freed slave.

1. Andreau and Descat, *Slave of Greece and Rome*, 99.
2. Davies, *Early Christian Church*, 213.
3. Beard, *SPQR*, 522.

PART 2: BELONGING

The Roman Senate seriously debated at one time having all slaves wear the same kind of clothing to tell them apart from free citizens. This idea was quickly dropped, however. It was pointed out that the slaves would then be able to identify each other as well. They would know how numerous they were (perhaps a third or more of the population in some urban areas) and be tempted to organize and rebel against their masters. The proposal was dropped. Still, there were other ways to tell just by looking whether someone was a slave.

You could usually tell that someone was a slave by the scars. The Romans, and others, whipped slaves for the most trivial offense or for no reason at all, simply to keep them in their place.[4] The whips they used often had bone or metal tips that tore the flesh so deeply it was not unusual for a slave to die from loss of blood or infection after a whipping. These beatings would leave terrible scars. Whippings were also common punishment given to any noncitizen found guilty of a crime. Although Paul was a Roman citizen, he was sometimes mistakenly whipped by local magistrates when his preaching caused a public disturbance (Acts 16:37; 1 Cor 11:24). For more serious crimes, noncitizens were tortured and then crucified. A citizen convicted of a serious crime would be beheaded (considered more humane). For example, tradition says Peter was crucified while Paul, being a citizen, was beheaded sometime around AD 64.

Most take Paul's words at the end of Galatians, where he refers to the scars he received, to be the result of being whipped and beaten for preaching about Jesus. "From now on let no one cause me trouble, for I bear on my body the marks of Jesus" (Gal 6:17). For "marks" he uses the Greek word *stigmata* which means "markings." Some have taken this word, however, to mean that Paul had not just the marks from being whipped but rather the marks in hands, feet, and side made on Jesus's body by his crucifixion. These *stigmata* could only be miraculously caused, yet there is nothing in the text to suggest this is what Paul meant. The scars from the whips were enough for Paul to share with Jesus.

Some early Christians were known to whip themselves to show their devotion and willingness to endure hardship for Jesus.[5] Christians generally disapproved of this practice, citing the fifth commandment which forbid hurting or harming your neighbor (which would also include yourself). It was also considered prideful, a type of boasting: "See how much I am

---

4. Andreau and Descat, *Slave in Greece and Rome*, 110.
5. de Wet, *Unbound God*, 22.

The Marks of Belonging

willing to endure for you, Lord!" Much later, in the monasteries, which were founded on the ideas of self-denial and self-sacrifice, it was still sometimes practiced. But if one were willing to confess Christ in a hostile world, as did Paul, there would always be others willing to make those scars for you. In the early church, scars were considered to be marks of one who confessed Jesus in the midst of their enemies, not marks you inflicted on yourself in self-denial.

As with Paul, confessing Christians have often had to endure scars and death. In the past year, I have read in the news of churches being bombed in Pakistan and India, of Christians killed or enslaved by radical Muslims in Africa, imprisoned and tortured in the Middle East, China, and other Asian countries, and of Christians losing jobs, families, and homes. In the West, scars are more likely to be social, economic, political, or psychological. No matter the risk, a slave of Christ is told to expect this kind of treatment, to accept the risk (Matt 24:9–13), and still be prepared to speak about Jesus (Matt 10:16–32). Jesus said, "If the world hates you, know that it has hated me before it hated you. . . . I chose you out of the world, therefore the world hates you. Remember . . . 'a servant is not greater than his master'" (John 15:18–20). Peter told us not to be surprised at the "fiery trial" when it comes "as though something strange were happening to you" (1 Pet 4:12). We are not to take persecution personally because it is really directed at Jesus, and they are only trying to get at him through us. Jesus considers the persecution of Christians, who are his body at work in the world, as persecution of himself (Acts 9:4). And so it his to avenge (Rom 12:14–21).

In the first century, the whipping of slaves was common, yet not all slaves were whipped. And even if we today escape the worst abuse, we must be in prayer and support for our brothers and sisters around the world who bravely continue to speak of Jesus under the threat of torture and death. There is an organization called The Voice of the Martyrs that seeks to help those who are persecuted for confessing Christ and to keep the rest of the world informed about their suffering and sacrifices. Other organizations within various churches try to do the same. By supporting them we share in their suffering as the body of Christ. "Do not be ashamed of the testimony about our Lord, nor of me his prisoner, but share in suffering for the gospel by the power of God, who saved us and called us to a holy calling" (2 Tim 1:8–9).

Slaves were marked in other ways than by whippings and scars. Among the Hebrews, a permanent slave (one who chose to stay when released) had his ear pierced with an awl, which would have been easily seen (Exod 21:6). In the rest of the ancient world, it was common to tattoo or brand a slave. Tattooing was more common in the East and branding was more common in the West, especially for difficult slaves.[6] In the East and in Greece (the former empire of Alexander), slaves would be branded or tattooed with the Greek word for slave, *doulos*, or, more commonly, just the first letter of that word, a delta, on the wrist and/or ankle. Since the Greek lowercase (minuscule) letters did not come into common use until the ninth century, this would have been a capital delta (uncial), which looks like a triangle.

Today, Coptic Christians in Egypt, a majority Muslim nation, wear the tattoo of a cross on their wrist or on the back of their hands to identify themselves as Christians. To avoid being accused of proselytizing Muslims, which is punished severely under Muslim law, many Coptic Christians will not allow people into their churches unless they can show their cross tattoo. I am not advocating tattoos. But just consider for a moment the possible witness in wearing a tattoo of the capital letter delta, as an ancient slave would have done. A capital delta looks like a triangle, also an ancient symbol of the Holy Trinity (see front cover). It could be an opportunity for a Christian to explain to others about how Christians are slaves of Christ and about the God we serve and why we serve. It could prompt questions or be a conversation starter that allows us to talk about our faith in Jesus. We could call it a mark of God's ownership, a witness to our baptism, that we belong to the triune God. Although it may not get us into any churches, it may open other kinds of doors for us.

The Romans, of course, took the marking of slaves one step further. In order to punish difficult slaves, they would brand a slave on the forehead, as a sign for everyone to see, with the word "thief" or "runaway" (or simply F or FVG for *fugitivus*).[7] They would also sometimes weld an iron collar around the necks of some slaves that bore the words "stop me I am running away." When archaeologists first discovered these collars, they wondered whether they were dog collars, but because of their size and inscriptions, it soon dawned on them that these were for people.[8] The negative stigma attached to tattoos, which were only for slaves, may explain why tattooing was not popular in the West until modern times.

---

6. Harris, *Slave of Christ*, 123–25.

7. Harris, *Slave of Christ*, 33–44.

8. Card, *Better Freedom*, 31, 50. He notes that "fleeing from our master" often describes us as well.

The Marks of Belonging

The idea of being marked, tattooed, or branded, especially on the forehead, as a mark of ownership is also found in the Revelation to St. John. This book is characterized by a series of visions about the last days of the world and the coming of Jesus in glory to rescue his people. Much of its imagery comes from the visions of Daniel, Ezekiel, and other Old Testament prophets. There is, however, one image that comes from John's world, the Roman world of slavery. In the Revelation, the idea of ownership is expressed by means of names written (tattooed, branded) on the forehead or on the hand. "Do not harm the earth or the sea or the trees, until we have sealed the servants [*doulous*] of our God on their foreheads" (Rev 7:3). God's name on the forehead marks you as belonging to him: "On Mount Zion stood the Lamb, and with him 144,000 who had his name and his Father's name written on their foreheads" (Rev 14:1).

You can also be owned by the beast: "It causes all, both small and great, both rich and poor, both free and slave, to be marked on the right hand or the forehead, so that no one can buy or sell unless he has the mark, that is, the name of the beast or the number of its name" (Rev 13:16–17). "And on her forehead was written a name of mystery: 'Babylon the great, mother of prostitutes and of earth's abominations'" (Rev 17:5). But for those rescued by faith in Jesus, "They will see his face, and his name will be on their foreheads" (Rev 22:4). "The one who conquers, I will make him a pillar in the temple of my God. Never shall he go out of it, and I will write on him the name of my God, and the name of the city of my God, the new Jerusalem, which comes down from my God out of heaven, and my own new name" (Rev 3:12). Without understanding the world of slavery, these references just seem strange to us.

God writes a new name on us. In fact, he writes his name on us, not just a label ("slave") but a name. Slaves did not have a name of their own. They were property, and each time a slave was sold their new master simply gave them a new name of his choosing.[9] Slaves were often given names like *Onesimus* ("useful") or *Philodespotes* ("master lover") in hopes that they would live up to those names. Slave names were often shortened into nicknames; Lucius became Luke, Demetrius became Demas, and so forth. You may remember that when the slave of a Roman citizen was freed, he would be enrolled under his former master's name as part of his new name.[10] He would bear his master's name.

---

9. Card, *Better Freedom*, 42–52.
10. Sherwin-White, *Roman Society and Roman Law*, 146. "The enfranchised person

Part 2: Belonging

Like slaves, God gives us a new name and a new family: "The nations shall see your righteousness, and all the kings your glory, and you shall be called by a new name that the mouth of the Lord will give. . . . You shall no more be termed Forsaken . . . but you shall be called My Delight Is in Her . . . for the Lord delights in you" (Isa 62:2, 4). "But his servants [*evadeem*, slaves] he will call by another name" (Isa 65:15). To express their changed relationship with him, you may remember that God also gave both Abram and Jacob new names. And then there is our new family: "See what love the Father has given to us, that we should be called children of God; and so we are" (1 John 3:1). But the one name we take for granted is perhaps the best of all: Christian—a slave of Christ.

In a far older sense, wearing the name of God or having his name put on you as a mark or "seal" of his ownership goes all the way back to the time of Moses. God tells Moses to "put his name on" the people of Israel with the words: "The Lord bless you and keep you; the Lord make his face to shine upon you and be gracious to you; the Lord lift up his countenance upon you and give you peace. So shall they put my name upon the people of Israel, and I will bless them" (Num 6:24–27). Even though it may not be printed or imprinted physically on your forehead (or on a birth or baptismal certificate) for everyone's eyes to see, these words "mark you as one redeemed by Christ the crucified." That phrase comes from the rite of baptism as the pastor makes the sign of the cross on the forehead and on the heart of the one to be baptized.

The blessing in Num 6 is a triune name put on the people with appropriate triune blessings: the Father, creator, and "keeper" (first blessing); the Son, who won us "grace" with a cross (second blessing); and the Holy Spirit, who with faith gives us "peace" (third blessing). It is the "seal" of God marking us as his property. It is the name put on our forehead when we are baptized. When we receive this blessing at the end of a service, it traces on us again our brand with the delta triangle representing our triune God. We may not be stamped, tattooed, or branded, but we are the baptized and the marked property of the triune God nonetheless. He has signed his name on us and signed his name on a personal promise to redeem the one baptized for Jesus's sake. We, too, bear on our bodies the marks of Jesus. (Gal 6:17).

---

commonly takes the first two names—*praenomen* and *nomen*—of his benefactor and retains his own original single name as a *cognomen*. . . . The enfranchised person is also formally listed as a member of one of the thirty-five Roman tribes."

TAKEAWAY

In this section we looked at what it means to belong to God. Although slaves were legally considered nothing but property, they were not objects. They were living persons, and as such, belonging must be considered as a relationship. The Bible uses three types of relationships to describe how we belong to God. In the marriage relationship, two people belong to each other in heart, body, and mind. This is both a formal (i.e., legal) and a personal (i.e., committed) union. In Christ, we are formally declared to be a part of his body, the church, the bride of Christ. He shares our sin, and we share in his righteousness. Personally, we are committed to him, submitting completely to him as our head (Eph 5:22–30). This is not a relationship of equals. God is the creator, and we are his creatures. What God has made, he owns. As his creatures we are dependent beings and will be happiest only in that relationship for which we were created, creatures belonging to their creator and doing his will, as we were designed to do. And finally, in our relationship to Christ as king, we are brought again to the issue of authority and obedience. Christians are "resident aliens" wherever we are on earth. Owned by our God-king, our primary allegiance and obedience is to Jesus, and we cooperate with worldly authority only where it does not contradict him (Acts 5:29).

How would you define marriage? Did this discussion change your view of it? In what way? In what way does it help (or hurt) your understanding of belonging? Do you see yourself as a "dependent being?" Why or why not? So far in life, what has made you the happiest? Does that tell you anything about your "design?" Why or why not? When you call Jesus your Lord, what do you mean exactly?

By baptism we are "born again" into God's family. Scripture describes conversion by comparing it to birth, which is why faith is not chosen, nor is it forced upon us (John 1:12–13). Like life itself, faith is a gift (grace) given by the Holy Spirit working through the word and promise that comes with the water of baptism. The distinction between child and slave in an ancient family may have been legally defined, but in actual fact, it depended on how the father of the family chose to treat you. In baptism God claims us as his own and we are both his purchased property and his adopted sons and daughters. The slave is treated as a child, and both children and slaves belong to the family. The master gives us a new name, his name. In baptism God "puts his name on us," Father, Son, and Holy Spirit (Num 6:24–27).

Did you choose to follow Jesus? What do you think now? Does it make any difference? What does birth into a family have to do with belonging? What do you think happens in baptism? Why? Why are names important?

Slaves could be identified by their scars and other marks, and so can Christians. Slaves were sometimes tattooed or branded with a delta, the first letter of *doulos* (slave), to identify them as slaves. The capital letter delta looks like a triangle, the symbol for the Trinity, and could be worn today by Christians to identify themselves as belonging to the triune God, a slave of Christ. Regardless of whether we bear any identifying marks, the name of God put on us in our baptism "marks us as one redeemed by Christ the crucified." Even if we can't see it with our eyes, we know it is there, and God knows it is there, and we can be sure that God will be true to his promise to be merciful to us for Jesus's sake. He has signed that promise with his name and faith holds onto it. If we reject it, insisting on our independence, it is useless. Only faith clinging to the promise in the saving work of Jesus, delivered in baptism and/or in the spoken message, will help us. It makes us a "new creation" (2 Cor 5:17), a member of his family and a member of his kingdom.

If you have any tattoos, why did you get them? Do you have any scars from following Jesus? What are they? What do you think a Christian should look like? Should people be able to recognize a Christian when they see one? How? Would you consider getting a delta (triangle) tattoo? Why or why not?

PART 3
Serving

"No one can serve two masters."—Matthew 6:24

CHAPTER 7

Work or Service?

"The kings of the Gentiles exercise lordship over them, and those in authority over them are called benefactors. But not so with you. Rather, let the greatest among you become as the youngest, and the leader as one who serves."
—Luke 22:25–26

IN HIS *SMALL CATECHISM*, Luther teaches us to say: "I believe that Jesus . . . is my Lord. Who has redeemed me, a lost and condemned person, purchased and won me from all sins, from death, and from the power of the devil; not with gold or silver, but with his holy, precious blood and with his innocent suffering and death, that I may be his own and live under him in his kingdom and *serve him in everlasting righteousness, innocence, and blessedness.*"[1] We are bought by Jesus. We belong to Jesus. We serve him only. We are his slaves. That is simply what Luther thought a Christian was.

A slave, then, must serve another. If we are to understand how we, as slaves of Christ, are to serve him, we must first change our entire understanding of work. There is an important disconnect between our modern understanding of work and that of the ancient world. Andreau and Descat in their book on slavery in Greece and Rome put it plainly: "The slave is, by definition, a subject being and his work represents the most powerful symbol of that subjection. This is all the more so since, in antiquity, work was viewed as a service, *a social relationship*, rather than an autonomous and individual activity, as in modern times."[2] In other words, we see work

---

1. Luther, Luther's Small Catechism, 17. Emphasis added.
2. Andreau and Descat, *Slave in Greece and Rome*, 66. Emphasis added.

as a task to be completed, an "individual activity," whereas they saw it as a service rendered, a duty performed for someone, a "social relationship."

To us, work is valued by how much gets done in a certain amount of time and how much we will get paid for it (paid by the task or by the hour). The operative word is "get." In this other view, work's value is determined by what is given to someone else, what is due to them because of who they are. The operative word is "give." Any payment received for a task was then a "reward" or an "award" from the one who received the service, an appreciation for a service given. Obligation was all one way, from the servant to the master, not the other way around. This difference is theologically important. In our worldview, good works should "earn" us heaven, but in their worldview, good works are given as part of a relationship. It shows appreciation and honor to the one who has first given us heaven. The master may show his appreciation and reward a faithful servant (Matt 25:23), but the master may choose to reward workers differently (Matt 20:13–15) or not at all. Remember, everything depends on the grace of the master.

Luther, in comments on Deut 8:17–18, describes why this difference is so important:

> When riches come, the godless heart of man thinks: "I have achieved this with my labors." It does not consider that these are purely blessings of God, blessings that at times come to us through our labors and at times without our labors, but never because (*ex*) of our labors; for God always gives them because of his undeserved mercy (*ex gratuita misericordia*). For, as we have said above, he uses our labor as a sort of mask (*larva quaedam*), under the cover of which he blesses us and grants us what is his, so that there is room for faith and we do not imagine that by our own efforts and labors we have achieved what is ours.[3]

We assume a mechanical cause-and-effect relationship between work and reward that was not taken for granted by the ancients. In the Sermon on the Mount (Matt 6:25–33), Jesus uses the example of the birds of the air to correct this misconception. Again, as Luther explains: "It is true that the bird doth neither sow nor reap, yet would she die of hunger if she flew not in search of food. For who put the food there, that she might find it? For where God hath put nought, none findeth, even though the whole world

---

3. Plass, *What Luther Says*, 3:1495.

were to work itself to death in search thereof."[4] God provides through our work but not because of our work.

Like the birds flying in search of food, people were made for work. This is part of the image of God, who loves to work, and which we reflect (John 9:4). We are not content unless we are busy with meaningful work. But work may or may not result in a blessing. The result is always a gift of God, "not a result of works, so that no one may boast" (Eph 2:9; see also 1 Cor 1:26–31). The farmer may plow, plant, and cultivate, but a storm could wipe out the crop. The factory workers may produce the best product, but no one may buy it. The laborer may be worthy of this hire, but this is not a guarantee that he will see any reward. Add to this that the one who hired you, who gave you the work, is free to reward you as he sees fit (Matt 20:1–16 or 25:14–30), and you will begin to "leave more room for faith."

Ideas of service, obligation, and duty held the ancient world together. In the Hebrew language, the verb for "work" is *eved*, and one might expect, therefore, that *eved* when used as a noun would mean "one who works" or "worker," but it does not. The noun form of *eved* is not "worker" but "slave." Zimmerli explains in the *Theological Dictionary of the New Testament* that when forming the noun, the "content of this verbal root is replaced by a specific personal relation . . . the *eved* is the 'worker who belongs to a master.' The whole rich development of the *eved* (slave) concept commences with this element of relationship."[5] Horace Hummel even suggests that the book of Job is primarily about this servant/master relationship with God and not about our modern ideas of suffering and justice.[6]

The Romans, of course, also viewed work as a service that depended on relationships. "Officium" was an expectation among friends or people of the same class or *status* (see below). It meant that this labor was to be exchanged, not paid for. Crook describes this as a "mutual serviceableness between *status*-equals."[7] If you did something for me, then I was to do something for you. If I represented you in court, then you would not pay me, but you would show your gratitude by giving me something or doing something for me in return. Doctors, for example, did not charge fees; they were instead awarded a gift of appreciation.

4. Bonhoeffer, *Cost of Discipleship*, 160.
5. Zimmerli, *Theological Dictionary*, 5:656–57.
6. Hummel, *Word Becoming Flesh*, 474–91.
7. Crook, *Law and Life of Rome*, 192.

Part 3: Serving

Of course, the ancients knew about and used contracts—so much money for so much work—but these were still understood as service relationships. "From all the principal Near Eastern societies, and from very early times, there survive contracts of labour, but those societies were characterized by the 'spectrum of statuses': few men and women were absolutely free, few were absolutely slaves, and labour contracts were an entry into some degree or other of personal subjection to the employer."[8] Contracts fit into their worldview of obligation, or as it was sometimes put, the universal system of bondage.

The Hierarchical Model of the Universe

Services were exchanged if you were of similar *status*, but services were always a duty owed by those of lower *status* to those of higher *status*. You were not necessarily paid or rewarded for this kind of service. Children, no matter their age, owed obedience (labor and service) to their fathers, slaves owed obedience (labor and service) to their masters, freed slaves still owed labor and service to their former masters, wives owed this obedience to their husbands, everyone owed obedience to their city or to the emperor, the emperor owed obedience to the gods, and the lesser gods owed obedience to the greater gods. In fact, everyone owed service and labor to someone, or to several someones, in a great hierarchical chain of service, obligation, and "bondage" to those above you. The only exception was the being at the top, the greatest of all gods.

Chis L. de Wet has described this hierarchy of service as a universal way of thinking in the ancient world. It was the way the universe worked.[9] Every physical and spiritual being had its place, purpose, and duty to another. This model can be found as early as the time of Plato and continued long into the Middle Ages. Everyone was under some form of bondage, under the power and authority of someone or something. Physical slavery was only one example of this, though of course at the lowest level of society, but everyone was in some sense a slave to another and owed service to them. Only God was "unbound," that is, unruled by another and free. As de Wet says, slavery was the model for all relationships, "a tool to think with."[10] Concepts of bondage, obedience, and service describe the order of

---

8. Crook, *Law and Life of Rome*, 94.
9. de Wet, *Unbound God*, 6–21.
10. de Wet, *Unbound God*, 147.

all things, "a very different worldview from that of most modern, especially Western, people," he observes.[11]

Since the Enlightenment and the industrial revolution, the modern model of the universe is the machine. All things relate to each other as parts of a machine. The solar system is a combination of "gears," orbits mathematically defined, not a system of "spheres" governed by degrees of power and authority as the ancients believed. Today the human body is a biological machine, not the incarnation of a spirit in which faith rules over reason and reason rules over the passions of the body. There is no "ghost in the machine." The brain is only a machine built of neurons. The world is an ecological machine with interacting parts, not a kingdom with a ruler that everything must serve in its proper place. In a machine world, control is the highest value, and science is the tool that has given man control over nature, making him a god, completely free to change anything he wants (even his own genes). This is the definition of freedom to a machine. Once at the mercy of the gods, then of the random changes of evolution, now man is finally gaining control even of his own evolution. Our first parents also thought that control, the freedom to choose, was real freedom. But, as we must always remind ourselves, the freedom to choose evil is not freedom; it is slavery to sin and death.

In the ancient worldview, no one was "free" in our modern sense. Our concept of independence (e.g., "no one can control me," "no one can tell me what to do," "I don't owe you anything," "I can do what I want," etc.) simply did not exist. In this older system everyone had a responsibility to serve those above them. When Christianity did away with the gods by replacing them with one God, it made little change in this way of thinking. In the feudal system, serfs served the lord of the manor, who served the nobles, who served the king, who served the pope, who served (and represented) the one true God.[12] This service was owed to your lord, even at the cost of your life.

To be a "masterless man," not accountable to someone, did not mean you were free. It meant you were either a criminal or a beggar. This is one example of why C. S. Lewis said that to understand the Middle Ages one

---

11. de Wet, *Unbound God*, 6–13.

12. Not all kings saw it this way. One of the biggest debates of the Middle Ages was whether the king was under the authority of the Pope and subject to obey him. When the hierarchy model was discarded, so was this debate. Thomas Hobbes and John Locke, with their social contract theory, simply did away with God and put all rulers under the authority of the people.

must understand this hierarchy of loyalty and duty, what he called the "discarded image." He called it a "discarded" image because we use a different model of reality today.[13] Mechanical or material evolution is the tool we think with now. Lewis observed that all models are human constructions and not reality itself, and so we should humbly recognize that "no Model is a catalogue of ultimate realities, and none is a mere fantasy. Each is a serious attempt to get in all the phenomena known at a given period, and each succeeds in getting in a great many."[14] There are bits of wisdom in every age which we can learn from because all models contain some truth. In this older system, all things in heaven and earth, peasants and kings, demons and angels, had their right place under the proper authority. Those who think they can throw out all authority in order to be free may still be able to learn something from this.

This older model also explains why some forms of work were held to be evil and were to be avoided (John 13:6–8). You had others "beneath you" to do those things. Especially in Roman society, everyone knew where they were on this scale because it was based on money and power, on things everyone could see. The kinds of service you performed, and especially for whom, were an indicator to everyone of where you "stood" in the world and told people who you were. And, of course, you wanted to appear as high on the ladder as you could. No one wanted to be caught doing the work of a slave (John 13:6–8).

Christianity, however, was going to make some fundamental changes in the system. For example, the early Judeo-Christian worldview gave a strange dignity to all forms of work. Genesis tells us that humans were created to work because they were created in the image of a God, who loves to work. Nothing was beneath you. Jesus even did the work of a slave, washing the feet of his disciples on Maundy Thursday, an example of the humble service he expected of his followers (John 13:1–17). He was obedient to the point of death, even dying the death of a slave on a cross (Phil 2:7–8; Matt 20:25–28). Doing things "beneath you" to help and serve even those of the lowest classes became, for a Christian, a public confession of faith.

There was a social cost for this ideal. Serving those beneath you on the social scale also made you look like a slave, those on the lowest rung of that scale. This was shocking, especially to non-Christians who did not understand why you would do such things. It did, however, greatly help

---

13. Lewis, *Discarded Image*, 216–23.
14. Lewis, *Discarded Image*, 222.

Work or Service?

Christians understand their new role, and with it, the expectation to serve. It seemed to them, at least, like a new position outside the usual social order that had great dignity.

By serving others, they were serving Christ (Matt 25:40). Pagan temples sometimes bought and employed slaves to help with their rituals, but being a slave of Christ was different. It wasn't providing a ritual in a temple but serving your neighbor. And it was also a surprisingly effective witness. "By this all people will know that you are my disciples, if you have love for one another" (John 13:35). The social standards of wealth and power and the pressure to fit in eventually determined that only "elite" Christians would humble themselves in this way, as we saw with the ascetic movement and the formation of monasteries.[15] Even so, in the first century, many Christians seemed to have had a more biblical value of work (Col 3:17) so that even doing the work of a slave (John 13:1–17) was not considered shameful but could be considered an honor (Col 3:24). Identifying as a slave of Christ would help explain their odd behavior of service and self-sacrifice, not only to themselves but also to those outside the church.

Even though this new *status* was eventually "spiritualized" into a metaphor and Christians began to adopt the old worldly categories again, it still had a continuing effect on Christian thought. G. K. Chesterton observed:

> Now it is the peculiar honour of Europe since it has been Christian that while it has had aristocracy, it has always at the back of its heart treated aristocracy as a weakness—generally as a weakness that must be allowed for. If anyone wishes to appreciate this point let him go outside Christianity into some other philosophical atmosphere. Let him, for instance, compare the classes of Europe with the castes of India. There aristocracy is far more awful because it is far more intellectual. It is seriously felt that the scale of classes is a scale of spiritual values; that the baker is better than the butcher in an invisible and sacred sense. But no Christianity, not even the most ignorant or perverse, ever suggested that a baronet was better than a butcher in that sacred sense. No Christianity however ignorant or extravagant, ever suggested that a duke would not be damned. In pagan society there may have been some such serious division between the free man and slave. But in Christian society we have always thought the gentleman a sort of joke.[16]

---

15. Davies, *Early Christian Church*, 276–79.
16. Chesterton, *Orthodoxy*, 125–26.

Part 3: Serving

Whether or not Chesterton is right about this attitude in Europe, Christianity never completely lost its revolt against the world's hierarchical system. Jesus said, "You know that the rulers of the Gentiles lord it over them, and their great ones exercise authority over them. It shall not be so among you. But whoever would be great among you must be your servant [*diakonos*], and whoever would be first among you must be your slave [*doulos*], even as the Son of Man came not to be served but to serve, and to give his life as a ransom for many" (Matt 20:25–28). Jesus turns the power pyramid of the world upside down.

Usually, your position in a power pyramid is determined by how many people are under you, by how many serve you, with room for only one at the top and the rest under him. But according to Jesus, greatness is determined by how many people you carry. The lowest point on this upside-down pyramid carries everyone above and serves them. Jesus is, of course, the one at the very bottom, or highest point on an upside-down pyramid, who carries us all, and he urges us to follow his example. This greatly simplifies the pyramid—Jesus on the bottom holding us up and we then holding up everyone else. The authority structure is reduced to two positions, the master (Jesus) and the slaves (us).

Most people, when they draw a pyramid, simply draw a triangle. As we noted before, the Greek letter delta, which looks like a triangle, was branded on the slave. It stood for the word *doulos* or slave. In Christ, human slavery is "stood on its head." As Paul said, "He is the head of the body, the church. He is the beginning, the firstborn from the dead, that in everything he might be preeminent" (Col 1:18). As our head, he lowered himself under the law, under our punishment, to carry us back to God. The delta can remind us of this too, and where we stand (or rather on whom we stand). We just need to remember to stand the delta on "its head" (pun intended). It would naturally look upside down to someone looking down at their own tattoo on a hand or a leg.

The ancient hierarchical pyramid of service may not be how we see things today, but the modern world still has a hierarchy. We now value power, dominance, and control instead of service, and so we still have "pecking orders" in modern society. The main difference is that we now understand this from an evolutionary model of the universe, no longer that of duty and obligation owed to greater beings. We have come to accept "survival of the fittest," or domination by the strongest, as the natural order. We don't owe anyone anything and we naturally step on them on our way up the pyramid. It is important for us to understand the more ancient way (Rom 13:8), to see it and use it, as Chris de Wet suggested, as a "tool to think with." Most of us still tend to think it is somehow better if others serve us, but this is where remembering who, or whose, you are may help.

It does not help that in our culture the concepts of "loyalty" and "duty" have all but disappeared. I can't remember the last time I saw those words in print or heard them used in a sentence. They survive only as attachments to our idea of love. For the people we love (it's not politically correct to love countries anymore) we will show something like loyalty and perform something like duty toward them, but the moment the emotion dies and we don't feel love for them anymore, all loyalty and duty are gone, and usually so are we. Marriage, child support, military service, these are not matters of duty but law. If they are not seen as opportunities for personal benefit, then they are only something forced on us. When loyalty and duty are tied to emotions, they must cease to exist, for these words are meant to describe a commitment that holds despite changing emotions.

Of course, love for God produces loyalty and obedience to him: "If you love me, you will keep my commandments" (John 14:15). But beware! Whenever the Bible uses the word "love," it is not referring just to a feeling. Love, *agape*, is a committed love, a complete self-surrender, a devotion that leads to sacrificing anything for the other. *Chesed* in the Old Testament is often translated as "steadfast love." The word "steadfast" expresses a commitment of the will. For example, God's *chesed* means that he is loyal to his promises. Even when his people deserve his anger, he treats them with grace. He sacrificed the life of his Son, and he will remember his promise to those who trust in him no matter what their sins.

There is no good English translation for either *chesed* or *agape* because in our culture love is only a feeling and has no sense of commitment, loyalty, or duty. Often it refers only to sexual passion, as in "making love." At best, something like "love of country" would only be a feeling of sentimental attachment. "Love of God" would be the same. Translating these words as "love" will only lead to misunderstanding. For example, when God feels hurt or angry and must punish sin, it is not because he has stopped loving us, but because he does. To many people, "tough love" is a contradiction in terms.

Perhaps it is best not to think of loyalty as coming from love but both love and loyalty coming from belonging. No, I do not mean the "feeling of belonging." If you google "belonging" that is all you will find. I mean the *fact* of belonging as dealt with in the last section. The husband that really belongs to his wife, children that really belong to their parents, citizens that really belong to their country, the Christian that really belongs to Jesus. There are many people who do not consider loyalty and duty to be good things or even desirable things (it gets in the way of "me first") and are genuinely puzzled when they see it. But the Christian who sees all things in the light of the cross will see loyalty and duty differently. We will see ourselves as the slaves of a wonderful master. We gladly belong to him. We are convinced that this is the best of all possible lives. So, whether we feel like it or not, we will "make it our aim to please him" (2 Cor 5:9). "Slave of Christ" is not just a tool to think with but also a tool to live by.

Chris de Wet observes that because this way of thinking affected all thinking in the ancient world, it also affected early doctrinal development, especially Christology, and not always for the better.[17] Christ, according to Phil 2, was like a human slave or like any child under the rule of his father, obedient and obviously a "bound" creature. Therefore, how could Jesus also be the "unbound" God? Applying the hierarchy of beings to God led to Arianism, which taught that Christ was not equal to God but a lower being on the scale. Naturally with the worldview of the time, this idea would be very appealing, and it took the church a long time to defeat it (though of course this idea still survives in Islam). Whether they realized it or not, the church fathers defeated this with the principle of Scripture alone. What Scripture said was true even above human reason. This important principle is made even more explicit in the Reformation when the issue is not the Trinity but the forgiveness of sins.

Our concern here is not, however, with early doctrinal disputes, but on how this worldview determined the way Christians saw themselves, and how it affected their actions. Here Chris de Wet observes that "Christians thought of themselves primarily as 'slaves of God' . . . and to them, this was not a metaphor. They believed that they were really under his power and belonged to God as they would belong to a human being."[18] This, he says, resulted in a "Christian ethos" or *habitus*, an identity with a strong sense of duty and loyalty. This *habitus* was to be characterized by humility, service, and self-control: humility in that they were to serve others, especially in

---

17. de Wet, *Unbound God*, 119–48.
18. de Wet, *Unbound God*, 9–13.

"doing things beneath them," and self-control in that they were to discipline their sinful desires to live virtuously for the honor of their master.[19]

Although I may seem to spend more time focusing on an ethos or *habitus* of service, it, of course, cannot exist without self-control and self-discipline. This *habitus* might also be understood in terms of a God-given desire for excellence—not only moral excellence but excellence in all our actions. Excellence can only be achieved by self-control and self-discipline, both gifts of the Spirit flowing from faith (Gal 5:22–24). Perfectionism is *not* a Christian ideal (Phil 3:12). But the pursuit of excellence *is* a Christian ideal. "Whatever is true, whatever is honorable, whatever is just, whatever is pure, whatever is lovely, whatever is commendable, if there is any excellence, if there is anything worthy of praise, think about these things" (Phil 4:8). Whether moral, occupational, or artistic, excellence is attempted for the master. It comes from a worldview in which all work is understood as service. Bach wrote *soli Deo gloria* even on much of his secular music because he believed he served God with all his music.

I have always admired the American Shakers for getting this right (they had so much else wrong). Their furniture makers, for example, believed that to make things well was an act of service to God. They not only took satisfaction in a job well done, but they also believed God did. They were simple, direct, hardworking, and honest (moral honesty, not the modern meaning of self-revelation or self-expression), and they made their furniture that way. They used the best materials they could find. Cheap material and poor craftsmanship were dishonest, even a kind of stealing or taking away what was due to another. They tried to make a thing strong, light, efficient, handy, and balanced, with little ornamentation (this was seen as prideful). They had an oft-quoted saying: "Don't make something unless it is both necessary and useful; but if it is both necessary and useful, do not hesitate to make it beautiful."[20] To live in service to Jesus with a life of moral excellence and with excellence in all that you do is to "walk in beauty," as the Navahos say. The Bible promises "whoever pursues righteousness and kindness will find life, righteousness, and honor" (Prov 21:21), or as Mic 6:8 describes it: "He has told you, O man, what is good; and what does

---

19. de Wet, *Unbound God*, 27–31. The concept of habitus comes from Aristotle, but Christians began to see it as something that is God-given, the Holy Spirit working through faith to sanctify us, or, in my terms here, to build a Christian character. See Fluegge, "How Is Theology a Habitus?," 3–31.

20. Porter, "Shaker Design Philosophy," para. 1.

the Lord require of you but to do justice, and to love kindness, and to walk humbly with your God?"

But here is the paradox. The building of a Christian character is not done by trying to build a Christian character. It is done by serving others, by doing what is "necessary and useful" for others. Character is not the result of self-denial or self-improvement but self-forgetting. It is formed by love found in service to others. Gifford Grobien explains:

> Love cannot exist except in relation to others. Consider the various catalogs of spiritual movements in the New Testament. They typically include fruit such as godliness, humility, love, patience, meekness, concord, hospitality, thanksgiving, and joy, among others. These are not mere personal habits which an individual exercises in an isolated way to improve his character, tempting him to pride in his accomplishments. Such movements and fruit take a person outside of personal interest into relation with others, both God and men. Godliness is right, humble submission to God's word and thankful, joyful, praiseworthy response to him. Love opens one up to the interests of those around him. . . . Truly good works always occur in relation to others, in the humility of the self before God and in loving fellowship with other Christians.[21]

In service of the master, we serve others ahead of ourselves, and that produces self-control, self-discipline, and the other virtues because they are the tools we need in order to serve. It is the only way to pursue excellence, as well as to do the right thing in our personal life and to do both with humility because we are not even thinking of ourselves. It is only possible through love, the love we receive from Jesus for unworthy sinners like us and then shared in what we do for other unworthy sinners.

When Christianity changed the power pyramid, turning it upside down and exalting service, it had an interesting side effect. Working as slaves to serve the same master made all slaves equal. When Christians were quarreling over opinions on food, holy days, and other things not specifically directed in Scripture, Paul says, "Who are you to pass judgment on the servant of another? It is before his own master that he stands or falls" (Rom 14:4). As long as both parties were seeking to honor the Lord in these "middle things" and not insisting on their own way and creating stumbling blocks for "the weak in faith," Paul was content to let them go their own way

---

21. Grobien, "Spirituales Motus," 330–31.

(Rom 12:1–12).²² Being slaves of the same master, one cannot tell the other one what to do without a word from the master. All slaves are equal. Even if one is appointed overseer, they are still only slaves with different duties. There are now only two positions left in the hierarchy, Jesus and his slaves. Work as service, or loyalty, to one master, Jesus, would have a profound effect on all the social structures that Christianity would encounter. Perhaps Chesterton was right. At the very least, ideas about equality will trouble the Christian conscience throughout history.

All in the Family

In one sense, the two-position hierarchy of master/slave, God/us, was not new. It was always a part of the Judeo-Christian understanding of both God and the family. The Hebrew Scriptures described our relationship with God as our heavenly Father and we as his children. Even though the Greek and Roman world had a complicated hierarchy of service in their society, the Greek and Roman family, like the Hebrew family, was only two-positioned. There was the father, *pater familia*, the master, and everyone else. As we have already noted, everyone in the family was under the father's complete control, very much like slaves.

Even in a two-position hierarchy, there must be one above the other. There must be an authority that is recognized and obeyed, someone to whom duty and service is owed. It has been the consensus of philosophers and sociologists throughout the ages that it is primarily by the family that a society's authority structure is built and/or maintained.²³ Even in the Ten Commandments, the first table starts with the authority of God and the second table starts with the authority of parents and government, delegated to them by the first. Many have noted the importance of fathers in modeling a child's first ideas about God (see Heb 12:5–11). If the family, even in some small way, determines a society's view of authority, then we have a problem.

The traditional nuclear family, a father, mother, and their children, is now the minority family type in America. Children are raised in very chaotic and shifting arrangements of adults and other children. Media portrays

---

22. In 1 Cor 10:23–24 we saw that *adiaphora* must be for the good of others. Not causing others to stumble and lose their faith is a specific example. The limit on not causing offense is found in Rom 16:17.

23. For example, see Chesterton, *Everlasting Man*, 53–55.

fathers as helpless, powerless idiots wandering through life, clueless and selfish. Media portrays women as strong, competent, and caring but also selfish, not "nurturing" or "mothering." These things are seen as threatening our independence. Parents in the media are either deadbeat parents who don't care or "tiger moms" or "helicopter parents," "smothering" their children. In any case, these parents are not giving the child the freedom and independence the child deserves. In other words, authority is seen as restricting the freedom and independence we all deserve. Because authority challenges our independence, it is has become a problem, a thing to be resisted, ignored, and not, as in the old system, a blessing to be honored and used according to God's design and purpose.

Whether broken families are the cause or the result of this anti-authoritarian view in our society is a chicken-or-egg question, and for our purposes, it matters little. We must recognize our dysfunctional relationship with authority, come to terms with it, and develop a healthier understanding of authority and response to it. Why? Because Jesus said: "All authority in heaven and on earth has been given to me" (Matt 28:18). To have a healthy relationship with Jesus, we must not only appreciate his love but also live under his authority. As we saw in the last section, in the ancient world, you are defined not by what you did but by who you served. This relationship defined you. If the foundation of all relationships is the family, then there is no better place to improve our understanding of authority than by considering what the ancient world, the world of the Bible, thought of authority, especially as seen in the structure of the family.

The birth of a child changes a couple into a family. The place of the child in the family might surprise you. The Greek equivalent of *eved* is either *doulos*, slave, or *pais*, a child. It might strike us as strange that "child" should be used to translate the concept of "a worker who belongs to a master," but that is exactly how children were seen, even up to very recent times. Children belonged to their father and were under his absolute power and control, often working alongside slaves and doing the work of slaves as soon as they were able.[24] St. Paul is only stating a fact when he says, "I mean that the heir, as long as he is a child, is no different from a slave, though he is the owner of everything, but he is under guardians and managers until the date set by his father" (Gal 4:1–2). In American slavery, male slaves of any

---

24. Crook, *Law and Life of Rome*, 98–139. The description of the Roman family which follows comes from this section.

age were often called "boy" just as in Rome, and this racist habit continued in America long after slavery was abolished.

There were no child labor laws until the nineteenth century, and every child did physically difficult tasks alongside grown men. In wealthy families they were treated no differently, but they were also trained to do what would one day be expected of their *status* or class. Until then, a child's master was their father or someone appointed by him (Gal 4:2), and they were expected to obey like a slave, or they were punished like a slave—though usually not whipped since the child of a noble Roman family had a different *status*. In most instances, however, the Roman *pater familia* owned, controlled, and disciplined his children like slaves.

The Roman father's power extended over his entire *familia*, which included not only wife and children but also any servants or slaves. Legally he had the right to kill any member of his household if he saw fit, but other than killing unwanted children and some runaway slaves, this was not often done. Sometimes legal formalities were observed (e.g., a trial by the father or a magistrate as judge depending on the crime). The children, even when grown, were still bound to obey their father. He could, and often did, tell them who to marry and to divorce if he felt it served his family's interests. The father also remained in complete control of all the family's property and money; his children could own nothing, no matter how old they were, until after his death. They could use their father's money under his direction, but it would not be theirs until after he died. This was, in practice, no different from the *peculium* for the slave (see below).[25]

In Gal 4:2 "until the date set by his father" does not mean until the child reaches legal age, as in our culture, since age had nothing to do with it. The date of emancipation could be set by the father at any age, or never. A father could, and sometimes did, emancipate or "disown" a child so that he could give him his own property or set him up in business. Disowning dealt only with property rights, however, and did not mean being put out of the family circle. If named in his will, an emancipated child could still inherit from his father. And even if emancipated, the child still had a duty of obedience to the father.

Slaves could never own property because, unlike the children, they *were* property. Still, like a family member, a trusted slave could represent his master in a business of some kind, and for this he was often given a

---

25. Crook, *Law and Life of Rome*, 56.

peculium, money entrusted to him to use on his master's behalf. If freed, a slave was often allowed to keep the *peculium* to start a new life.

While emancipation was the term for freeing a child from under the authority and control of a *pater familia*, freeing a slave was called "manumission." Freed slaves, however, were still considered to be part of their former master's family, and though legally free were still under the same obligation of obedience as other members of the family. Remember that if the master was a Roman citizen, the freed slave would also become a Roman citizen. This was a highly prized benefit of being the slave of a Roman citizen. Still, because of his continuing obligation to his former master and family, a freeman would often still be referred to by others as "so and so's slave." A freed slave was never a social equal or ever considered of the same *status*.

In the first century, a person's place in the world was determined by the idea of *status*. *Status* was your legally and socially defined position in the social hierarchy. It had little to do with your nationality, ethnic group, or where you happened to live. John Crook explains how different this is from our world. To understand that world, he says, one must "think himself back into a world where men's rights and duties depended on a fundamental difference of status."[26] Crook then explains:

> Thus, if you had visited the market-place of, say, Tarsus in the time of the apostle Paul you would have found there Roman citizens, citizens of Tarsus (some of whom would be Roman citizens as well, like Paul, others not), citizens of other places domiciled but only having the rights of *incolae* [a permanent resident] there, and free persons who were not citizens of anywhere. Of all these, some would be free-born, others freedmen, some independent, others under the power of fathers or guardians. And the rest of the population would be slaves. Each kind of person would be carrying round with him a different bundle of rights and duties in the eyes of Roman law.[27]

In this list, Crook lumps all slaves together in one legal class, but he could have kept going with all the differences among slaves: rural or urban slaves, prisoners and condemned slaves working in the mines or rowing the galleys, agricultural workers or trained artisans, household domestic slaves or slaves in management positions, professional slaves like doctors,

---

26. Crook, *Law and Life of Rome*, 36.
27. Crook, *Law and Life of Rome*, 37–38.

accountants, bankers, teachers, or municipal slaves working in or managing city government, imperial slaves belonging to the Emperor and working in the imperial "civil service," or any number of other possibilities. Which kind of slave you were did not affect your legal *status*, but it did make a great difference in the way you were treated and in the conditions in which you lived.

Some slaves, like the managers of a wealthy household or those in civil service jobs like tax collecting, could even become quite wealthy and control large sums of money or property, and even own slaves themselves. These slaves of a slave were called *vicarei*, a slave in place of a slave, who substituted for you by doing your job or perhaps even taking your punishment.[28] The money they controlled was a *peculium* that belonged to their master, but if they were freed because of faithful service (as sometimes happened, especially at the death of their master) they could expect to take a large amount of this *peculium* with them. We will come back to the *peculium* when we look at the role of the steward in the next chapter. A slave could be many things to many people and have any number of different kinds of relationships with others, but the legal relationship of the owner and the slave who served him never changed.

Authority in the family, then, was understood in the ancient world as absolute and complete power belonging to the father. Since there were only two levels or positions, everyone else was in the other position, whether slave or free, under him. This did not mean that there were not loving and close families—there were no doubt many. It was just that they functioned with a different idea about authority—one that the Bible also assumes in its discussion of our relationship with God. Certainly, Christians today cannot legally organize their own families this way. We probably would not want to even if we could. It is, though, a helpful way to understand our relationship under God's authority as members of his family. We must not only understand it; we must, out of love and loyalty to our Savior, work at surrendering to his authority no matter what our own experience has been.

Understanding the authority of the father is also helpful in understanding prayer. Luther describes prayer as asking God "with all boldness and confidence . . . as dear children ask their dear father."[29] Respecting the authority and the wisdom of the father makes it very difficult to see prayer as "magic"—using the right words to get God to do what you want, like a

---

28. The obedience and death of Jesus in our place is called the "vicarious atonement."
29. Luther, *Luther's Small Catechism*, 19–20.

"spell"—using prayer as an attempt to control God. People who say "I tried prayer and it didn't work" look at prayer that way. Instead, confident of his love and respecting his authority, we end our prayers with "not my will but thine be done." We accept his position as the one who calls the shots, knowing that as our "dear father," he will respond to us out of love with what is best for us. He is our father, and we should talk to him like our father.

CHAPTER 8

What Does Service Look Like?

> "By this all people will know that you are my disciples,
> if you have love for one another."—JOHN 13:35

IN THE LAST CHAPTER we had to correct the idea that work is a task done for our profit. It turned out to be a service done for others. In this chapter we will have to correct another idea, that all our activities can be seen as either "sacred" or "secular." When we use "slave of Christ" as a tool to think with, it gives us another way to see things. Our modern idea of sacred and secular began in the Middle Ages with the monastic movement creating a special religious class of people doing "religious" things and normal people doing normal or "secular" things. During the Enlightenment era the ancient philosophic idea of gnosticism, the separation of the physical world and spiritual world, was added back into our thinking. Concern with the physical world then became the realm of the "secular" and concern with our internal world (mind, ideas, imagination) then became the realm of the "sacred." As we have seen, this made it quite easy to be a "spiritual person" and not have it influence your behavior at all.

J. G. Davies, in writing about Christians in the first century, describes their world differently. For them, he wrote, "Worship is not just one element amongst many in the life of believers; it is rather an attitude or orientation that should characterize the whole of it. So, in the New Testament there is no essential distinction between worship and life; man's existence is not split into two areas, one where Christ is honoured and the other where man is more or less independent—everything should stand under the Lordship of Christ."[1]

Many modern people tend to have very strange notions about what it means to be religious. They may think a slave of Christ, for example, would mean "doing religious things" all the time—like praying, reading their Bibles, preaching, helping the poor—and nothing secular—like going to work, shopping for groceries, mowing the yard, hanging out with friends. C. S. Lewis observed:

> Before I became a Christian, I do not think I fully realized that one's life, after conversion, would inevitably consist in doing most of the same things one had been doing before, one hopes, in a new spirit, but still the same things. . . . Christianity does not exclude any of the ordinary human activities. St. Paul tells people to get on with their jobs. He even assumes that Christians may go to dinner parties, and what is more, dinner parties given by pagans. Our Lord attends a wedding and provides miraculous wine. Under the aegis of his church, and in the most Christian ages, learning and the arts flourish. The solution of this paradox is, of course, well known to you. "Whether ye eat or drink or whatsoever ye do, do all to the glory of God." All our merely natural activities will be accepted, if they are offered to God, even the humblest, and all of them, even the noblest, will be sinful if they are not. Christianity does not simply replace our natural life and substitute a new one; it is rather a new organization which exploits, to its own supernatural ends, these natural materials.[2]

We must forget the notion of sacred or secular just as we earlier rejected the difference between a scientific and a religious reality. There is only one reality, in which all things belong to God and are to be used for his glory. The garbage collector is serving his neighbor and has a holy calling if he seeks to honor God where God has put him. The teacher, delivery man, CEO, construction worker, or preacher all work under the same calling, to love and serve God by loving and serving their neighbor. This is the "new organization" or "orientation" both Lewis and Davies referred to and the *habitus* or "way of living" that de Wet described. Today we tend to use the word "vocation" for this calling to serve God and our neighbor in our occupation with the talents and abilities he has given. A vocation can be any God-honoring occupation where we can show our love for him by serving

1. Davies, *Early Christian Church*, 57.
2. Lewis, *Weight of Glory*, 23, 25.

others (1 Pet 4:10–11). And, as we saw in the last chapter, it doesn't matter whether we get paid for it but only who we do it for. Mother and father are not paid positions, but because we serve God and our neighbor, they are sacred callings or vocations. As we show God's love to others we should always be "prepared to make a defense to anyone who asks you for a reason for the hope that is in you" (1 Pet 3:15–16). Service gives us an opportunity to "show" our love for Christ and "tell" who we are doing it for.

Character

By now it should be clear that service is a heartfelt response to the saving lordship of Jesus, shaping one's entire life, view of the world, and our life in it. Sometimes we talk about someone's Christianity as being only "skin deep" (other phrases are "nominal" Christian, "carnal" Christian, "worldly" Christian, etc.). These phrases are meant to describe a "weak" or "immature" faith. All faith in Christ brings forgiveness and life, no matter how weak. But faith that is weak is fragile and easily destroyed by the situations of life (Matt 13:20–21). Being fed and watered by God's word, faith, like a seed, over time should sink its roots deeper into all areas of our lives. Without attention and tending, however, there are no roots, and it stays "on the surface" of life. Thinking of yourself as a slave of Christ is a very "rooted," mature understanding, affecting all areas of our lives (Eph 3:14–19; Col 2:6–7). As a *habitus*, it is the way of seeing and responding to everything in our lives with Jesus Christ as Lord. Modern words we have considered for this *habitus* are "Christian identity" or even "character."

As already suggested, Christian character is formed over time through a discipline of loving others as Christ has loved us. Only the Holy Spirit can give us that kind of love, but as for what this love should be doing, Scripture has much to say. We can, with the help of God's word, focus on specific areas of life that will help us to grow into being more mature Christians, into being better slaves of Christ. But before we consider a few of these, we should review a couple of warnings about how easy it is to lose our way when not listening to the voice of our shepherd and why it is important to always be guided by God's word.

As we become aware of other people's needs and how we can meet them, serving others will inevitably lead to self-sacrifice and self-denial (Luke 9:23). Because God has promised to take care of our needs, generosity is a natural response for a follower of Jesus (Acts 2:45; 2 Cor 9:6–11).

But, as noted before, there is a danger in generosity and self-denial. They can easily become not just an expression of our trust in Jesus and a way to help others but an end in themselves. We think self-denial and generosity make us "holier." We begin to think that the greater our self-denial and generosity the better God will love us, ignoring this important fact: we are loved by grace alone, not because of our works. God's word on this is clear. Take some classic examples.

Celibacy and abstinence are sometimes thought to make us "holier," but this ignores God's designs for marriage and our use of creation (1 Tim 4:1–5; 1 Cor 7:2; etc.). Giving up or giving away "worldly things," as if all material things were evil, ignores Eph 4:28, 1 Cor 16:2, 2 Thess 3:12, 1 Tim 5:8, 2 Cor 9:6–11, etc. It's the love of money, not money itself, that is the "root of all kinds of evil" (1 Tim 6:10). Some forget that "go, sell what you possess and give to the poor" (Matt 19:21) was directed to one specific individual (with one specific problem) and is not a command to us all, nor, if it is done, does it merit any reward or special holiness with God (1 Cor 13:3). All of us are commanded to work so that we can financially take care of ourselves (2 Thess 3:12) and our families (1 Tim 5:8). The idea is to manage our resources God's way, not get rid of them.

The danger with self-denial is that it can lead to ignoring God's real will for our lives and lead to self-righteousness and pride. This does not mean we should give up on self-denial and generosity but only that we should watch ourselves and be on guard. Seeing ourselves as slaves of Christ, owning nothing and deserving nothing, will help. But it's hard not to feel proud about being humble. Mayer reminds us, "The Christian life cannot be viewed atomistically, as though it consisted in observing certain canonical hours, exercising oneself in specific virtues, performing certain prescribed works. . . . The Christian life is 'new obedience' in whatever sphere of activity the Christian finds himself. . . . The Christian devotes his service entirely to God and to his fellow man and is never prompted to seek his own welfare."[3]

Celibacy and voluntary poverty may not be issues to many people in our modern world, but there are two challenges in our world that make having a serving relationship with our neighbor difficult. I am referring to the areas of sexuality and how to treat our enemies.

Paul speaks specifically to sexual immorality: "You are not our own, for you were bought with a price. So glorify God in your body" (1 Cor 6:19–20).

---

3. Mayer, *Religious Bodies of America*, 174.

What Does Service Look Like?

Being a slave of Christ, bought at the price of his blood, we use the gift of sex only within marriage, which is the will of our master. Today, the confusion of sexual identity and the homosexual agenda requires a whole separate treatment, which we cannot do here, but Christians should study God's word about our sexual lives carefully. We must seek to please Jesus above all else and not use sex as a way to abuse others. Sex is meant to be a blessing in the committed relationship of marriage. The damaging effects of sex outside of marriage on relationships and health are well researched. Sex without the committed relationship of marriage is psychologically, sociologically, and theologically a form of abuse. The first Christians knew this and were strikingly different in their sexual behavior. "In Imperial Rome, the Christian view of sex proved revolutionary. . . . Early Christians held marriage sacred and asserted the full humanity of little children. . . . Christianity's teaching on sexuality blew up the pagan death star. Now, via the sexual revolution, the empire has struck back."[4] First it separated sex from childbearing, then both from marriage, and finally the distinction between male and female. Slaves of Christ will seek to honor God with their bodies—yes, even in our modern age.

Our world is also divided into hostile camps with hatred and anger increasingly expressed in many ways towards those who disagree with us. This is sometimes referred to as "the culture wars." When we feel attacked, it may help to remember the example of the first Christians. Eusebius, the church historian, was an eyewitness of how Christians acted in AD 311 when, during persecution in the time of Diocletian, Christians were brutally tortured and killed. But then when a great famine and plague began to kill thousands, Christians cared for the sick and tried to feed the starving when everyone else closed their doors to them. They cared for the very people who had earlier been screaming for their blood. This was a very powerful and effective witness that changed the attitudes of many toward Christianity.[5] Compassion for those who hate us is, of course, modeled for us by Christ himself (Luke 23:34). Though it is hard to care for the sinner behind the sin, remembering that it is not about us but about God's care for all sinners through us will help. If we keep the focus on Jesus and not on us, it is easier to remain compassionate. Our actions must speak louder than our words. This is the best response to hostility.

---

4. Scaer, "At Home in the Body," 65.
5. Mayer, *Eusebius'* The Church History, 328–29.

Part 3: Serving

Beyond these difficult areas in today's world, the Bible gives numerous examples of how our sacrifice and service can work within a very "normal life." These are all areas in which our maturity can grow as love for Christ moves us to "conform to the image of his Son" (Rom 8:29). In this, I think it is especially helpful to look at the parables, many of which just happen to deal with slaves. These provide some good examples of the kinds of principles that can govern our service and make them God-honoring and not self-honoring. Of course we are not to be limited by these examples. In his words and actions, Jesus gave us many examples of serving. But the parables are the stories Jesus used to illustrate his main points when preaching. And so, parables about the kingdom of God that talk about slaves are a good place to start a more detailed look at service and what it may look like. We can learn from these how we can serve in his kingdom.

Common Labor

Jesus used a variety of different kinds of slavery in his parables. The first to come to mind are parables about common laborers, some of which could be slaves, some not, but this does not change what it teaches about service. Among the most familiar of these are the parable about a farm worker, the sower (Matt 13:1–9), and the parable about a shepherd, the lost sheep (Luke 15:1–7). These highlight some important themes for us. Both are about workers who could be either slave or free but who have a high sense of duty. One has a job with no immediate prospect of success, sowing seed, while the other has a job that requires him to expend a lot of effort, perhaps even risk his life, for what many would consider a worthless object, a lost lamb. But there is more. When Jesus explains these parables, we find that a similar sense of duty, commitment, and caring can be used in the kingdom of God.

The sower is sowing the word of God. Servants of Jesus should be constantly and indiscriminately talking about Jesus ("sowing the word") to anyone and everyone (see Deut 6:6–9). That modern parents do not even talk to their children about their faith has resulted in a great loss of young adults to the church in our generation. And not talking about our faith in other public interactions has resulted in ignorance, misinformation, and cultural backlash ("bad press") against Christianity, and the loss of many others to the faith. Not only should we be talking about Jesus with those around us, but we should also be seeking, like a shepherd, for opportunities that may be an open door for talking about Jesus with others. Those who belong to Jesus should be actively talking about Jesus, thinking about ways to work him into conversations, and seeking opportunities to make him known.

Here we run into the problem of what the psychologists call "congruity." It is a simple idea, though not so simple to achieve. It means that what's on the inside of a person is what you see on the outside in the way they talk and act. They are "genuine," "comfortable in their own skin," "up front" with you. These are psychologically healthy people. The expectation in our culture is that Christians are to keep their convictions to themselves (inside only) because expressing them makes other people uncomfortable. This is a form of persecution. If we buy into this, it will damage us, our families, and our society. If others are free to share their views, there can be no objection if we respectfully do the same. If they object to our existence, then that is their problem, not ours. They never seem to worry about making Christians uncomfortable. We need to regain wholeness and congruity. As I said, it is not a simple thing to achieve. It will cost us honesty, repenting, and reforming—hard work—but worth it. G. K. Chesterton once observed that in a sinful world most good things will happen only after a lot of pushing against the current. As he put it, "A dead thing can go with the stream, but only a living thing can go against it."[6] Slaves of Christ will be countercultural. We don't try to be—we just are.

In the parable of the unforgiving servant (Matt 18:23–25), we run into the problem of congruity again, this time forgiving as we have been forgiven. In the Lord's Prayer we ask God to "forgive us our sins, as we forgive those who sin against us." People who live in the world of cheap grace do not forgive others. The automatic forgiveness found in cheap grace does not sit well when it's we who are sinned against. We find it hard to say it doesn't matter or that those who hurt us did nothing wrong. That's only what we say to ourselves when we have done something wrong. But if we are sinned against, we want payback. At that moment we see the forgiveness of cheap grace for what it is, or rather, what it isn't. Real forgiveness is rare; it stands out like a light in the darkness or a city on a hill. That is why it should characterize a slave of Christ.

In fact, I think it is probably true that only Christians can really forgive. Only a Christian can release the sinner from punishment and any personal need for revenge because the Christian has someone else to hand

---

6. Chesterton, *Everlasting Man*, 256.

it to. We don't have to stuff it and carry it around in our guts as anger. We can entrust the one who sinned against us to God and know that he will deal with the situation. It is no longer our business. I do not need to worry about competing with others (Matt 6:25–34) or about getting back at someone (Rom 12:17–21). I can trust God to take care of these things. Choosing not to hurt someone in return for the hurt they have given us is the definition of forgiveness. It is the way God expects us to forgive others. Doing this confirms that we believe Jesus has done this for us, and therefore we are able to do this for others. It makes us congruent. In fact, this allows us to see any conflict as an opportunity to "trust in the Lord, and do good" (Ps 37:3). We can leave the outcome to God, and we, instead of seeking to win or pay back, can work to see that justice is done, that help and care is given to others, and so give glory to God.[7]

Some New Testament words for forgiveness are *aphiemi*, "to let go" or "release," and *charizoomai*, "to bestow favor freely or unconditionally." God does not want us to hold on to anger and bitterness but to let go of them by surrendering every hurt to God and trusting that he will deal with it (1 Pet 5:6–7). Faith is trusting God to take care of everything, not just our sin and guilt but everything in life. This is also a reason we do not pray as we should, because we don't have a faith big enough to trust God for everything in life. But real trust is not selective. We should look at "in God we trust" as an absolute with no exceptions or fine print (Ps 56:4).

Yes, in the psalms, David prays that God would punish his enemies, and that does not sound like leaving it to God to deal with. But they are not just David's enemies. Because they are doing evil, they are also God's enemies. When someone injures God's property—and we are God's property—it is not the property which responds but the owner! "Beloved, never avenge yourselves, but leave it to the wrath of God, for it is written, 'Vengeance is mine, I will repay, says the Lord'" (Rom 12:19). Notice that with his prayer, David is actually putting his enemies in God's hands and not seeking personal revenge. Slaves must let the master deal with these things. We prevent what damage we can, but without being given more authority, we must let God, and his appointed authorities, punish. This allows us to trust in the Lord and do good. Thinking of ourselves as slaves of Christ is especially freeing and helpful in these situations.

---

7. Sande, *Peacemaker*, 17–59. I summarize and adapt in what follows many of his points.

What Does Service Look Like?

People have many strange ideas about forgiveness. For example, they think that forgiveness is saying "It's OK," or "It was nothing," or "Everybody makes mistakes." Those are excuses, not forgiveness. Some think, "If I forgive you, I guess I have to like you now." Forgiveness is not a feeling; it is a choice. I may still be angry and still be able to forgive because forgiveness is an act of my will. I choose to release someone from liability to me, from punishment by me, and instead commit them to God to deal with. My job is to do what's best for them. That may be to ignore them, confront them, call the police, or some other act of tough love. We may need to take an injury to an earthly authority who is responsible by God's design to protect and defend those wronged (Rom 13:1–7). Even when turning someone over to God's representatives, I must still release an offender to God ("forgiving your brother from your heart," Matt 18:35).

When someone does not want forgiveness from those they have hurt or from God (repentance), I cannot proclaim them forgiven (Matt 18:17–18). I must forgive from the heart, but I can't be reconciled with them or pronounce them reconciled to me or to God without repentance. In fact, I may need to take steps to protect myself from further harm from them. But when there is repentance, I can begin the process of reconciliation and rebuilding the relationship. By seeking to honor God in our conflicts we find things not only work better but that this also gives a powerful witness to a faith based on our own forgiveness.[8]

The parables of the laborers in the vineyard (Matt 20:1–16) and the unworthy servants (Luke 17:7–10) teach us about humility, which was always noted in ancient times as the most important virtue of a slave. The laborers in the vineyard are not slaves. They are working for pay. But they fail to understand work as service. Instead, it is all about "what's in it for me." Because they are envious and greedy, they complain about the workers last hired getting paid just as much as themselves. But the master explains that they are being treated fairly because they all got paid what they were promised. If you remember what was said about work and service in the last chapter, this will make more sense. The reward depends on the master, on the relationship between master and workers, not on the task.

The "hired hand" was looked down on in the ancient world because he was working only for the money. He cared little for the quality of his work or for pleasing his master. Jesus doesn't have a high opinion of a hired hand in John 10:12–13 either. Work for pay in Latin is called *merces*, from which

---

8. Sande, *Peacemaker*, 204–23.

we get the word "mercenary"—as negative a word then as now. Aristotle considered those who worked for pay the equal of slaves.[9] He looked down his nose at those who did not understand work as service but were only interested in money. From this worldview, those hired first in the parable made a terrible mistake. They valued money over the master. When a father holds a quarter tightly in his fist and a child pries open his hand and runs off delighted with his treasure, he does not realize that the quarter will soon be gone and that the real treasure is the hand of his father, who can give him many more. The child, like the hired hand, is interested only in what he can pry out of the hand of another instead of the far greater value of one who can supply all his needs. The master takes care of his workers. They all receive a living wage, and that is more important than the issue of fairness. The generous master is the real treasure.

This parable can also lead us to a very different question: what is the purpose of wealth? The wealthy Greek or Roman valued money because it meant power, position, luxury—as it does for us. But they also believed wealth had a greater purpose. Wealth freed them to work at what they really wanted to do, to pursue their own interests, and help others pursue interests that aligned with theirs (patronage). They were not the "idle rich." They called this financial independence to pursue their interests *otium*. "The Romans regarded *otium* as an essential part of life, as opposed to *negotium*, which was the world of business and political and worldly engagements. *Otium* was seen as a time for personal research, study, creativity and contemplation, which was fundamental to the well-being of the individual and consequently of society as a whole."[10] It represented not only power over their own time, but also an obligation to be useful.

The rich built public services, roads, buildings, arenas, fountains, and forums. They studied and wrote on their favorite subjects, served in the senate, governed provinces, served as magistrates of various kinds. They tried to improve their farms and farming techniques. They supported clients, people who needed their support for new business ventures or to gain office. They understood it to be the duty of the wealthy to serve not only their family but also their city and their people. Sophocles was only repeating a common belief when he has the chorus in *Oedipus* say, "Ambition

---

9. Mirowsky, "Wage Slavery or Creative Work?," 73. He quotes Aristotle, *Politics* 7.9.2011b and 8.2.2011c.

10. Pezzo, "One Word," para. 3.

must be used to benefit the state; else it is wrong, and God must strike it from this earth."[11]

Of course, wealth and power were abused for selfish aims, just as with us. But unlike us, there was an expectation in their culture that wealth brought with it a civic duty to aid the community—even if seen as a way to gain the praise of others. It was still an honor they considered worth spending their fortunes to achieve. Christians have a far better reason to use wealth for the good of others: "As for the rich in this present age, charge them not to be haughty, nor to set their hopes on the uncertainty of riches, but on God, who richly provides us with everything to enjoy. They are to do good, to be rich in good works, to be generous and ready to share, thus storing up treasure for themselves as a good foundation for the future, so that they may take hold of that which is truly life" (1 Tim 6:17–19).

In our world no responsibility comes with money. Money is to buy us the things we think will make us happy and to give us the independence to avoid work and do nothing but entertain ourselves, which is our idea of "leisure." Genesis 2:15 gives us a different picture of work and rest. "The Lord God took the man and put him in the garden of Eden to work it and keep it." The verb here rendered "put" is interesting. It has the sense of Adam being set down or put to "rest" (another meaning of the word) in the garden. This cannot mean inactivity because the very next thing said is that Adam is to work it and keep it, or perhaps better, to preserve it. The sense of rest is that he was completely settled there, calm and at peace, free from worry and trouble. This is meant to contrast with the trouble and rest-less-ness of work after sin came into the world. The garden is a perfect fit for him; it is where he belongs, doing what he is meant to do, and what he enjoys doing. When we are doing God's will and serving our neighbor, we are living the life we were meant to live, a life that is "truly life." Busy with what God has given us to do is the secret of an "abundant life."

Besides using this parable to consider the role of work and wealth, there are still other ways to understand the parable of the vineyard owner. Some have understood the reward of the master (God) in this parable to be eternal life. In that case, it reminds us that everyone who serves Jesus receives the same reward of eternal life at the end of life, no matter whether they served him for a lifetime or for only a few hours. The classic example of this is the thief on the cross next to Jesus in Matt 19:23–30 who received

---

11. Sophocles, *Oedipus Tyrannus*, 20.

the gift of salvation just before his death. God gives all who trust in Jesus a "living wage."

You might also understand this parable as a lesson about envy. We are forever comparing ourselves with others and coming up short. The result is often envy, greed, pride, discontent, self-pity, and anger, just as with the workers hired early in the day. The point of receiving the same reward, then, is to underscore the point that all slaves are equal. Slaves have only what the master gives them, whether it seems fair to us or not. But it will always turn out to be "sufficient" for us (2 Cor 12:9). The master may give more to some slaves than to others, but what the master gives others is not our concern. He knows what he is doing. It serves his purpose in running his household and, because we are sure of his love for us, we know it will always be "enough." As Paul says, "I have learned in whatever situation I am to be content. I know how to be brought low, and I know how to abound. In any and every circumstance, I have learned the secret of facing plenty and hunger, abundance and need. I can do all things through him who strengthens me" (Phil 4:11–13). The result of understanding your position as a slave of Christ is contentment in any situation.

The inequality of what is given, the gifts and abilities among Christians, is explained in just this way: "Now there are varieties of gifts, but the same Spirit; and there are varieties of service, but the same Lord; and there are varieties of activities, but it is the same God who empowers them all in everyone. To each is given the manifestation of the Spirit for the common good" (1 Cor 12:4–7). There are many forms of slavery, many ways to serve, but we are all serving the same master. One way of serving the master is not better than another. The purpose of different gifts is like the different parts of the body that, although they are different, work together "for the common good" (1 Cor 12:12–30).

A slave of Christ must not compare himself or herself to others or live to impress others (1 Thess 2:4). The goal is to please only Christ. We perform for an audience of one. Everyone else may "boo" so long as he applauds. What others applaud, we may ignore.

Joseph was the slave of a wealthy Egyptian named Potiphar, and when Potiphar's wife propositioned Joseph, commanding him to have sex with her, Joseph only considers what God would think. God's opinion is all that counts. He says, "How then can I do this great wickedness and sin against God?" (Gen 39:9). Joseph performs for an audience of one. And Paul reminds us in 1 Cor 6 that even our sexual lives are to honor the one who bought us. We must not make decisions based only on what's in it for us. We serve another master. He gives us gifts for the common good.

No matter what gifts you are given, humility, especially "doing something beneath you," is required of those who work for Jesus. As C. S. Lewis suggested, this is more than charity. Giving money or material aid is important when there is a tragedy, but service is meant to be a giving of oneself. It is good to give to those in need, but it is far better to befriend them. Humility is thinking how you can do what is best for someone else. Thinking of yourself as a slave of Christ is a great defense against all kinds of pride and selfish temptations. The last parable in this group we are considering makes this point quite clear.

The parable of the unworthy servants in Luke 17:7-10 makes a good summary of this group of parables. It ends with "so you also, when you have done all that you were commanded, must say, 'We are unworthy servants [*doulos*, slaves]; we have only done what was our duty'" (Luke 17:10). Slaves get no credit for doing what they are told to do. A slave obeys; it is his duty. Because there is no choice but to serve, there can be no credit for doing it. Choosing agents deserve credit for making good choices. They make themselves righteous. But if a slave is, as Aristotle said, a "living tool," then there is no credit for the tool (see Rom 6:13). The person using the tool gets all the credit. We praise the carpenter, not his saw.

I cannot read Acts 9:15 where Jesus says about Paul, "he is a chosen instrument of mine to carry my name before the Gentiles," without thinking of Aristotle's definition of a slave as a living tool. He is an instrument, a tool, but a "living" one, with heart and mind changed by God's Holy Spirit into a thankful and willing tool, serving God with his whole heart. Paul said he was the "foremost of sinners" (1 Tim 1:15) and the "least of all the apostles" (1 Cor 15:9), yet he adds "to me ... this grace was given, to preach to the Gentiles the unsearchable riches of Christ" (Eph 3:8). Here again we see both the fear and love of God. You can hear regret in those words, but far greater is the joy in those words, a heart changed by the good news. "God's love has been poured into our hearts through the Holy Spirit who has been given to us. For ... God shows his love for us in that while we were still sinners, Christ died for us" (Rom 5:5-6, 8). Paul is an instrument, in his case maybe even a power tool, driven by love to honor God with his body.

Here, again, we must be wary of pride. The Christian is not righteous because he does righteous things. Luther objected to the Roman Church's understanding of righteousness because it came from Aristotle and the Greek philosophers and not the Bible. Rome had accepted the philosophical, and very logical, idea that in order to be good we must do good things. Grace then became the gift of a power from God to be righteous and so be saved. But a sinner can never be righteous enough. Luther stressed an "alien" righteousness, grace as a gift of righteousness from God, not a power to be righteous.

The Bible teaches that we are always sinners and are only accounted righteous for Jesus's sake, as a gift, and thus saved. Christians do righteous things not to become righteous, but because they belong to a righteous God, who, for Jesus's sake, declares them righteous. God holds us lovingly in his hand, like a tool, and uses us for a righteous purpose as we serve those God has given us to serve—spouse, children, family, employer, employees, etc. Who gets the credit? The master. Who does the work? We get to. We have to say we "get to" because it is a privilege to serve this master and through our work or vocation be used by him to bless those around us, even as we have been blessed. Some may question whether service is ever a privilege. The work may be demeaning, and we may get no credit for it—after all, it's slavery. But just consider the type of master we serve. In Luke 12:37, his servants, while waiting for their master, are busy with their tasks and ready to open the door when he comes. Jesus says: "Blessed are those servants [*doulos*, slaves] whom the master finds awake when he comes. Truly, I say to you, he will dress himself for service and have them recline at table, and he will come and serve them."

When Jesus washes his disciples' feet (John 13:1–17), he explains that he is among them as one who serves and who will lay down his life for us. And remember the "wedding feast of the Lamb" in heaven (Rev 19:6–10), where he will "dress himself for service and have them recline at table, and he will come and serve" us. "No eye has seen, nor ear heard, nor the heart of man imagined, what God has prepared for those who love him" (1 Cor 2:9). It is a privilege to serve such a generous master—especially when we remember that we are nothing but "unworthy servants (slaves)," and yet he treats us like family.

Stewards

The next group of parables we will consider do not deal with common laborers but with slaves who serve as overseers of their master's other property, including other slaves. The *oikonomia* (house manager) or *epitropos* (overseer) was given authority over some or all of the master's property.

What Does Service Look Like?

They were often responsible for the supervision of other slaves and property, deciding on tasks and putting slaves to work, rewarding and disciplining them to improve production, storing resources, accounting, calculating expenses, and making budgets.[12] They ran the household or they ran a business for the master, and in order to do so were given the money and power even to make contracts in the master's name.[13] The overseer was the limited legal representative of his master but was also strictly accountable for his actions.

In Old English the word for this person would be "steward," from the words *sty* or *stig*, meaning "hall," and *weard*, meaning "keeper," since he was the keeper of the master's hall (or his property). Abraham sent such a slave, entrusted with a large amount of Abraham's very valuable property, to find a wife for his son Isaac and to negotiate a bride price. Many consider him to be the Eliezer of Gen 15:1–6 since he is described in Gen 24:2 as "the oldest of his household, who had charge of all that he had." He was an excellent steward and always had his master's welfare at heart.

An example of a bad overseer is described in the parable of the wicked steward or the dishonest manager in Luke 16:1–12. When his mismanagement is about to be discovered, he "cooks the books" in favor of his master's debtors so they will feel obligated to help him when he is kicked out of his master's house. He doesn't simply try to take the money and run like a thief would have done. He was smart enough to know that if he did that, he would only be hunted down. Instead, he uses his master's money to buy himself some friends. Jesus commends him because he sees money as a tool that can be used for a smarter purpose, that it doesn't exist just to be enjoyed. That the money belongs to the master adds comic interest to the story, and it is meant to be a comic story with a serious point. We are not to horde money (God's money, after all) for ourselves but use it for a more important purpose, to make friends for God's kingdom.

Similarly, in the parable of the wicked tenants in Matt 21:33–44, the tenants want the master's vineyard for themselves and so kill the master's son. Even though this parable is clearly about the Jewish leaders wanting to kill Jesus, there is still an important stewardship observation. The only way we can claim that our possessions belong to us, that they are our own, is to "kill" God. We must eliminate his Son from our lives and take what is his as our own. Remember what C. S. Lewis said about us wanting to think

12. Andreau and Descat, *Slave in Greece and Rome*, 71–72.
13. Crook, *Law and Life of Rome*, 241.

of ourselves as independent and being our own masters? The irony is that even if we get rid of God, the things of this world will never be ours, and God is not disposed of so easily.

Being a slave of Christ is the best way to understand what we call Christian stewardship. If you remember, a slave (or child for as long as his father lives) can own no property; everything belongs to his master. A slave (or child) is only entrusted with things in order to manage them for the master. In the parable of the talents (Matt 25:14–30; Luke 19:12–37), some have tried to make the talents stand for a particular thing—the gospel, our abilities, or even simply money—but the talents include literally everything. "What do you have that you did not receive? If then you received it, why do you boast as if you did not receive it?" (1 Cor 4:7). The slave is expected to use the money or property entrusted to him, his *peculium*, as his master would want, with the goal of using it or expending it for the benefit of the master and his household. He has freedom of use but not ownership. The Christian is in the same position with God.

From a Christian worldview, the idea of owning property while at the same time not owning property can be problematic. For example, in Acts 2:42–47, Luke tells us that "the believers had all things in common." Is this statement describing some form of communism among the early Christians? Later, Luke helpfully explains that "no one said that any of the things that belonged to him was his own" (Acts 4:32–35). If you read this closely you will see that to *say* your things "are not your own" is not the same as not owning them. It means they held their property at the disposal of other people's needs. Their property belonged to them—that is, it was theirs to care for—but they freely shared it with others in need "as if it were not their own" (see 1 Cor 7:29–31). This is not a form of communism but generosity, acting as God's representatives, using God's priorities, to manage the resources he entrusted to our care for his purposes.

The problem with trying to understand ownership is that we tend to leave God out of our understanding of property completely. The seventh commandment, "you shall not steal," assumes private property, that there is something that belongs to another that can be stolen. But biblically (Ps 50:7–15), this "belongs to" means only temporary custody—responsibility for and control over, like a *peculium*. God owns everything and entrusts some of it to us to take care of, and that includes our obligation to use it to take care of others. It is not ours. As the old saying goes, you will never see a U-Haul behind a hearse. "For we brought nothing into the

What Does Service Look Like?

world, and we cannot take anything out of the world" (1 Tim 6:7). There is nothing wrong with the idea of private property if it is understood as "temporary custody," but often these issues of ownership are just another word for greed, and Paul reminds us that greed is idolatry (Col 3:5). Anything that replaces God is an idol, especially if it happens to be something we can call "mine." It is when we think of ourselves as slaves of Christ that we get stewardship right.

In an ancient household, the *oikonomia*, those who have been put in charge of the master's goods, must see to the needs of the other slaves in the household. That is their office, one of the reasons they are given a *peculium*. They also, of course, must use what they are given to take care of themselves and their own family as well as the other members of the household. In God's household, the priority is to liquidate resources to care for the needs of other people. People are more important than things, a priority taught in the commandments. Bishop Fulton Sheen famously observed that man was created to love people and use things, but after the fall into sin, man now uses people and loves things. Because we are sinful people, we must constantly reshape our priorities.

The *oikonomos* remains responsible for carrying out his master's wishes, not his own. And this principle of stewardship not only applies to the stuff of life but also to the church. Paul said, "This is how one should regard us, as servants of Christ and stewards of the mysteries of God. Moreover, it is required of stewards that they be found faithful" (1 Cor 4:1–2). It was perhaps a happy choice to use the Latin root word "peculiar" in the older English translations of Luther's Catechism in the section called the Office of the Keys: "The office of the keys is that *peculiar* authority which Christ has given to his church on earth to forgive sins."[14] "Peculiar" now means "odd or strange" and has been updated in recent translations to "special authority." But the old word has some advantages. The word "peculiar" shares the same root as *peculium*, the property of someone else used as your own, given for you to use in the master's place. In the Office of the Keys ("keys" from Matt 16:19 but understood from 18:18 and John 20:22–23) we recognize that forgiveness of sins belongs to God alone, it is his property, but he has given Christians permission to use it as our own, as our *peculium* when we represent him. Just as a slave could represent his master in a business or contract matter, a Christian can pronounce the repentant sinner forgiven and the unrepentant sinner still in their sin.

---

14. Koehler, *Short Explanation*, 275. Emphasis added.

Repentance is another word that has changed meaning over time. It now means to feel sorry when you do something wrong. But the Hebrew word for repentance means to "turn around," to turn from a sin to find God's forgiveness in Christ and then continue on in the right direction. When a sinner turns from sin to Jesus, seeking his forgiveness, a Christian can declare them forgiven "in the stead and by the command" of Jesus. It is like the *oikonomos* who represented his master in a legal contract, for as with the steward we stand in for the master and therefore can pronounce a sin forgiven "as if Christ our dear Lord dealt with us himself."[15] The contract is binding. When the Christian forgives a repentant sinner in the place of Christ, they are forgiven. It is a fact the forgiven sinner can count on and find comfort in.

In his stead, by his command, and in his name, we also baptize. In his stead, by his command, and in his name, we offer those attending the Lord's Supper (notice the possessive—it belongs to him, but we use it) the same body and blood Jesus offered his disciples on Maundy Thursday with the same words Jesus spoke to them, "given and shed for you for the forgiveness of sins."[16] The master has commanded us to do these things and say these things on his behalf, when and where he has commanded, and so as obedient slaves, we do them and we say them. But because we are only his representatives, we use them only as he directs. We speak the law to everyone but the gospel only to those who want God's forgiveness (Matt 7:6). We baptize "all nations" (Matt 28:19), no matter their age, ability, or standing, if they want themselves, or infants under their care, to receive faith and forgiveness for Jesus's sake. We take communion only with those who "recognize the body and blood of the Lord" under the bread and wine for the forgiveness of sins, as St. Paul tells us to do (1 Cor 11:27–32). These things are the *peculium* of the church, or, if you will, our "peculiar authority," entrusted to Christians to use as God directs.

Since Christians represent Jesus as his priests (1 Pet 2:9) or go-betweens with the world, proclaiming what he wants proclaimed, we could answer the question of what this service looks like by simply saying it looks like Jesus. The Christian's life is described in Eph 5:1–2 this way: "Be imitators of God, as beloved children. And walk in love, as Christ loved us and gave himself up for us, a fragrant offering and sacrifice to God." Then read from there to the end of Ephesians to find out what he means by walking

---

15. Luther, *Luther's Small Catechism*, 27.
16. Luther, *Luther's Small Catechism*, 29. See also Matt 26:26–28.

in love. There is no end of ways to show that he bought us, that we belong to him, and that we serve him "in everlasting righteousness, innocence and blessedness."

TAKEAWAY

The ancient world operated with a very different idea about work and service than we have today. It was a world of obligations, not rights. It was a world of service owed to those above you in a hierarchy of authority. Everything was in bondage to something or someone. The concept of slavery was, in this worldview, a "tool to think with." The first Christians altered this hierarchical system of obligation but did not do away with it. Instead, they reduced it to one master, God, and under him, all his slaves—equal and obligated to serve their master (Rom 14:4). Serving him was understood to mean pursuing excellence (moral and vocational) while at the same time serving others, deliberately doing things "beneath you" in true humility. Jesus turned the power pyramid on its head with the highest one serving the lowest one. Slavery can still be a "tool we think with." Although the idea of an upside-down pyramid survives as a Christian ideal, the world now uses a different hierarchical system based on power and control. Living with this upside-down worldview means Christians will do very normal things differently. For this reason, a slave of Christ will be seen as "different," not "normal," and even "countercultural."

Which pyramid are you climbing? Climbing up or down? How can you tell? How can others tell? In what areas of your life do you need to pursue excellence? Why would you want to? How will you do it? What would help? What does using slavery as tool to think with mean to you? Would you describe your life as countercultural? Why or why not? When would this be the most difficult for you? What might you do differently?

The parables Jesus told teach us about what service to our master might look like. The real difference is, of course, not in what we do but who we serve. It is all for Jesus. We must work toward congruence, or an agreement between our inside and our outside, our faith and our actions. For example, we will be helpful, but helpful will also mean directing people to hope and peace in Jesus. We will talk about Jesus, especially with those we love. We must not be intimidated into silence. On the other hand, in humility we must be careful not to personally judge others. Though honesty may require us to share the truth of God's law with others, we must stress that the same law also condemns us, and we, like them, find forgiveness only in Jesus. In that regard, the slave of Christ practices a sort of unreasonable

What Does Service Look Like?

forgiveness, forgiving as we have been forgiven. In this way also we find congruence between our words and our actions. Practicing forgiveness gives glory to God and is a witness to the way God forgives us, but it also frees us from bitterness and anger. Not only are we forbidden any personal judgment, we are not allowed to compare ourselves with others, but we are to keep our eyes only on our service of Jesus (Rom 14:1–12). Humility rejects an attitude of entitlement (my rights, what I deserve), and replaces it with, "How can I serve God and my neighbor?" It is self-forgetting. Since God takes care of us, we can concentrate on doing what is right and doing what is best for others, even in our conflicts. We can trust God and do good.

How are you doing at being congruent in words and actions? When is that hardest? When is it hardest not to compare yourself with others? What can help? Are you holding on to a grudge? How can you be free of bitterness? What is your understanding of forgiveness? Did you find any ideas in this section helpful? Which ones? Think of an example of a conflict you have had with someone, and rethink how it might be turned into an opportunity to glorify Jesus and do good.

The parables are a good place to learn about the different responsibilities given to slaves. Some slaves were stewards of their master's goods, which involved taking care of his business and other slaves. As stewards, we recognize that all things belong to God, who has entrusted us with managing them as best we can for him. We try to do with them what God would want us to do with them. We use them to care for our needs (both spiritual and physical), for the needs of our family, and then for the needs of others. People always come before things. Stewardship also applies in the church with the things of God. We do what he thinks the church should be doing, not what we or others think the church should be doing. The church is about delivering forgiveness of sins by calling people to Jesus (Matt 28:19–20). In doing this, we represent Jesus. We are his body, his hands and feet, at work in the world.

In what area of your life do you resist the idea of God's ownership the most? Do the people in your life always come first? If not, why not? What would this look like? What changes might you consider? If you are a member of a church, how do you think your church is doing as a "steward of the mysteries of God?" Is there anything you can do to help?

In our age when we are struggling to find our Christian identity, it is often said that the Christian life is more about "who I am rather than what I do." This is correct as far as it goes, but there is more. "Who am I?" is a modern question. "Who do I serve?" is a first-century question. They might conceivably lead to the same answer, but they are not the same question. Only the second comes from a biblical point of view (Matt 6:24). Who you serve determines who you are (Rom 6:16).

PART 4

What Does This Mean?

"I press on to make it my own, because Christ Jesus has made me his own."
—Philippians 3:12

PART 4

CHAPTER 9

Something Better

"Come to me, all who labor and are heavy laden, and I will give you rest. Take my yoke upon you, and learn from me, for I am gentle and lowly in heart, and you will find rest for your souls. For my yoke is easy, and my burden is light."
—Matthew 11:28–30

Does it even make sense to talk about slavery in the twenty-first century? As we have seen, when one human being owns another human being, it destroys them both. As Gregory of Nyssa said, it violates the order of creation, but it is worse than that; it also violates the first commandment. It is man playing God, usurping a position that does not belong to him but only to his creator—and he is a jealous God. When man plays God, he becomes a devil (Gen 3:5; John 8:44). The only way to talk about slavery in the twenty-first century, then, is in the context of Christianity, and then only where God is the master, in his rightful place as creator, Savior of all, owner of all, ruler of all. There can be only one master. But in that context, "slave of Christ" can be an insightful, helpful and even inspiring term.

Since the term "slave of Christ" was taken literally by Christians for only a short time before it was turned into a metaphor, the history of this word since then has been largely negative. It was twisted this way and that in preaching and writing. It was either understood legalistically, which is *not* the same as literally, and lost all the comfort and joy of belonging and serving, or it was watered down to mean a sentimental "Uncle Tom" sort of general kindness toward others, losing its radical insistence on obedience to Jesus. It stayed hidden under the label of *adiaphora* so that sinful men could use it to abuse other men. It is hard to get past this history. But that does not mean it isn't worth the effort to reclaim it.

The apostles and the first Christians saw something in Christianity that we often miss. If Jesus was who the prophets said he would be, and if he was who he said he was, then by his cross Jesus has purchased and won us from sin, death, and the devil so that we might belong to him, live under him in his kingdom, and serve him eternally. That makes us his slaves. Not the abusive, ugly kind, found in human slavery, but slavery nonetheless. Slavery could be washed of its sinful corruption (or "baptize" the word) to describe our relationship with creation's only master. If you think of it as a metaphor, you will miss its power to change the way we see ourselves and the way we act. When Paul said he was a slave of Christ, he did not say it with grim resignation but with a smile. This relationship is far better than its only alternative: being a slave of sin, death, and hell. In fact, it is the only way to an abundant, joyful, contented, fulfilling life.

The Alternatives

The alternative to belonging to Jesus is not pleasant. If there is no God, or if we live as if God did not exist (which amounts to the same thing), and if we accept a materialistic philosophy (religion) like evolution, then we are nothing but animals. The only purpose of an animal is to survive as long as it can until it can reproduce and pass on its genes and die. Like animals we find food, shelter, and safety by doing anything from hunting to working on an assembly line. Work's only purpose, then, is to survive. Life's other purpose is a few moments of pleasure. So along the way we seek pleasure (comfort, entertainment, sex) and avoid pain until we die. Animals are on their own, completely alone, living a pointless and brief life. "Every man for himself and devil take the hindmost." If our instincts are right and our consciousness somehow continues after death, then this existence after death must be an even more reduced state, a spirit without a body. We are still on our own, completely alone forever, without God and without hope of anything better.

This is our fate without Jesus. But we were made for something better, and all humankind has this instinct. We were meant to be the creaturely companions of the creator and enjoy him and our fellow creatures in a perfect world. This is what was lost, what was broken. Our first parents sinned and ruined it all. I don't think we often stop to consider what sin is and what it has done. I used to live in Michigan near the auto plants, so let me explain it using an analogy.

Imagine an assembly line worker on a line making cars. Each car slowly went by several stations where workers were responsible for adding or connecting each component of the car. One worker, whose job was to connect the steering gear to the front axle, had to go to the bathroom very badly but didn't want to stop the line. So right after connecting one gear, he ran to the bathroom and came back thinking he had made it just in time for the next car. But he did not. One car had gotten through without having its steering hooked up. The rest of the car was built with everything else in its right place. It looked great, shiny and brand new, and the engine ran perfectly. When a worker got in to drive it out of the factory, he could not steer, and the car crashed into the doorframe and smashed its front end. Now the question is, was it broken when it hit the wall or was it broken before it hit the wall?

Most people think sin is when you hit the wall and break commandments, but that is only the result of being already broken from birth (from the factory). Sinful actions are only the symptoms of the disease, the result of a sinful and already broken heart, which we inherited from our first parents. We had no connection with God. And this rebellion of our parents didn't just break all their descendants, it broke everything else in creation (Rom 8:20–21). The universe is falling apart. Stars explode and rocks crash into planets. Earthquakes, volcanoes, and other disasters tear the earth apart. The cells in our bodies age, mutate into cancers, and our organs fail. Everything dies. Everything is broken and nothing works as it was created to work. This is what sin is.

A radical problem requires a radical solution. A holy God could have turned away from his ruined creation and let it die, destroy itself and disappear. But God wanted something better for us. Because of his great love for us and for this ruined creation he became a part of it. He took on human flesh and lived among us. He did not come to teach us to do better. That would not work. We had a bigger problem. You can't teach a broken part in a car just to do better. And it wasn't as if someone could crawl under a car with a wrench and replace a part. The damage had been done, and more damage was continually being done. We were broken and getting more broken all the time. We needed more than a patch job. The thing that was breaking us had to be killed. Rebellion, a heart turned away from God, sin, had to be killed, and all the damage it had caused had to be paid for and repaired. He had to take us through a complete rebuild, a resurrection from the dead, and put us in a world where we would never get broken again.

This is why he came as one of us. He took our place under the law, under the obligation to be perfect and holy in thought, word, and deed. He did that for us. He took our place under the punishment due to imperfect and unholy sinners, dying with it and killing it in his now human body. He did that for us. We know that he has done everything necessary for our rescue, and we trust him to finish the job through the death of our broken bodies and the death of this broken world so he can rebuild us in the resurrection of the dead and put us in a new world, like the one we lost only better, where we can live with him in everlasting righteousness, innocence, and blessedness.

This was God's radical solution, and it calls for a radical response. As we have seen, faith is not a matter of knowing the right things about God and what he has done for us. Faith is trusting God, trusting that he will do all that he has promised, trusting that he died to make me his own and live with him forever, trusting that I belong to him and that I am meant to serve him. I am born without a connection to God, but his Spirit at work through the message of who he is and what he has done has given me the power to believe it, trust it, and live it. He has already started to rebuild me from the inside out, though that won't be finished until the resurrection. I am still broken, a saint and sinner at the same time, but God will do what he has promised (Phil 1:6; Heb 12:2).

Now the purpose of my life has completely changed. It is no longer to survive as long as I can and enjoy a few pleasures. As Robert Browning wrote: "Others mistrust and say, 'But time escapes: / Live now or never!' / He said, 'What's time? Leave Now for dogs and apes! / Man has Forever.'"[1] God has something better for us. There is comfort in belonging to the one who created you, who suffered the cross and death for you. There is contentment in finding your place in the universe and trusting a master who watches over you, who guides you with his word, who "knows my needs and well provides me." When children in a loving family are given strict boundaries, they feel secure, relaxed, and happy. In the same way, when we recognize the limits placed on us as creatures of a loving creator, we discover how to relax without worries for tomorrow (Matt 6:25–34). We feel secure knowing the wisdom and the power of the one who loves us. We are content and happy being what we were created to be.

---

1. Browning, "Grammarian's Funeral," 91.

Something Better

We cannot change the fact that we are creatures. The idea of freedom as having no limits, that we are in control and able to do whatever we want, is a lie, or worse. Because this cannot exist in the real world, it is a form of insanity. C. F. Keil called this "the imaginary liberty of the sinner."[2] And yet, as fallen creatures, it is our "default" or "factory setting" to believe it. It is the false dream we inherited from our first parents Adam and Eve. Even though science has allowed us to overcome many limits, it is irrational to assume that it can overcome every limit (though some, against all evidence, believe this by faith and make science their religion). We obviously live in a finite world, even though we have not yet discovered how far our ability to change the world can yet go. There is a limit to what one can do with matter and energy. And if we live in a moral universe, where good and evil have consequences, then, as with the law of gravity and other physical laws, consequences cannot simply be ignored. When broken creatures have the freedom to do as they please, misery and self-destruction are assured.

To be a human creature is to be limited either by the "elemental things of the universe "or by the ideas and "philosophies" we think with (Col 2:8). No one is free in an unlimited sense. We are slaves either of God or of our fallen nature, slaves of the creation (nature), of what is finite, passing away and dying. We are either slaves of good or of evil, of life or of death. The choice is not between freedom and slavery but rather whose slave you will be. Paul warned us to not be deceived about the alternatives: "See to it that no one takes you captive by philosophy and empty deceit, according to human traditions, according to the elemental spirits of the world, and not according to Christ" (Col 2:8).

Belonging to Christ is, on the other hand, truly freeing in a variety of ways. Believing, for example, that nothing I own is really mine is quite liberating. I can hold everything with an open hand—not clutching, grabbing, fighting to hold on to it—not destroyed and depressed when it is taken from me—but free to use each thing for its intended purpose and letting it go if need be. We have forever. The early church understood this and practiced it (Acts 2:42–47). Possessiveness and greed are the cause of much of our unhappiness. The Buddhist response to this "attachment" to things is to kill all desire and treat the world as something imaginary. The Christian response is to view the world as a *peculium* that belongs to another but is given us to use wisely on his behalf. A first-century slave would understand this without having to be told. Stewardship of all earthly things in service of

---

2. Keil and Delitzsch, *Commentary on the Old Testament*, 1:95.

our loving master Jesus reduces anxiety and worry, and results in contentment. It is a better way to live.

Also, when I understand my position as a fallen creature, redeemed by Jesus and now his slave, my relationship with my fellow fallen creatures becomes much more realistic and "workable." I do not need to compare myself to them, feel hurt when they do not meet my expectations, or be shocked at their failures. "There, but for the grace of God, go I," we say. Pride and judgment are replaced with humility and compassion. Even if, because of my sinful heart, I struggle with compassion, I will still act compassionately, not because of my ability to love but in response to a God who loves me. Remember, service always implies a relationship and not just a task. We have been "bought at a price" and have a debt of love to repay (Rom 13:8), an obligation to the one who set us free. That is helpful to remember when someone is making your life miserable at that moment. A freed slave had an obligation to serve the family that freed him, just as all members of the family had an obligation to serve the father. Sometimes when we serve very difficult people, we must remind ourselves that we are not doing it for them but in obedience to Jesus.

It helps to remember that we are not machines acting out of legalism but redeemed creatures trying to love as we have been loved. We strive to serve God "with righteousness and purity forever." This is not perfectionism; it is life under the cross. None of us can be a perfect slave. The first of Luther's famous ninety-five theses reads, "When our Lord and Master, Jesus Christ, said 'Repent,' he called for the entire life of believers to be one of repentance."[3] We sinners will struggle with sin our entire lives in this world. But this does not mean sin does not matter and that we don't need to strive to do God's will. Sin hurts, destroys, and kills both us and those around us. It is poison to be avoided at all costs. The freedom that leads us to choose sin is not freedom at all but only bondage to sin. It does not lead to a better, happier life; it leads to pain, suffering, and death. And so, we constantly turn away from it as often as it appears in our lives, turning back to God for forgiveness and strength to do his will. Repentance is the tool God uses to make us grow more like Christ. It does not make us perfect, but it does make us God's forgiven and holy children. Another thing it does, however, is make us humble slaves who can live humbly with our fellow sinners.

The Big Book of Alcoholics Anonymous describes repentance as an "inventory." The first step in AA is to give up on your own ability to change

---

3. Luther, *Ninety-Five Theses*, in Dillenberger, *Martin Luther*, 490.

and trust that God will change you. But if you are to avoid sliding back into drinking, *The Big Book* advocates the practice of regular inventory. This involves looking at your life for where you have hurt others (producing guilt) and where others have hurt you (producing anger, helplessness, and fear). These are the "backdoors" that will lead to drinking again, and in the sinner's case, will lead us to return to the same sins again. *The Big Book* then has great advice for sinners: "This is not an overnight matter. It should continue for our lifetime. Continue to watch for selfishness, dishonesty, resentment, and fear. When these crop up, we ask God at once to remove them. We discuss them with someone immediately and make amends quickly if we have harmed anyone. Then we resolutely turn our thoughts to someone we can help."[4] This is also how one moves from being the slave of sin to being a slave of Christ. Notice how this process ends. Instead of obsessing about your sin, you are told to find someone else to help.

Mahatma Gandhi famously said, "The best way to find yourself is to lose yourself in the service of others."[5] Gandhi often said he admired the teaching of Jesus, though he never became a Christian. Still, his observation captures the sense of something Jesus said, though he misses the reason. Jesus said, "Whoever loses his life *for my sake* will find it" (Matt 10:39, emphasis added). Like all service, serving others is because of our relationship with Jesus; it is done for him because of what he has done for us. This puts the motive, the purpose, the meaning, and, most importantly, the joy back into this kind of service. It is a "get to" instead of a "got to." Putting other's needs ahead of your own is strangely freeing and satisfying. Gandhi understood that, even if he didn't understand why. But we who follow one who went to the cross for us understand the "why" perfectly. The sacrificial service of others is the *telos* of a life lived in service of the one who sacrificed everything for us. *Telos* is the Greek word meaning the "goal" or "fulfilling the purpose" of something. Jesus used it on the cross when he said, "It is finished" (John 19:30). He did not say "I am finished," but "My purpose has been accomplished." That purpose was our salvation. He lived and died for us. And our purpose is to live and die for him and then live forever with him.

It is worth saying again that our obedience to him and our service of others is to be guided by God's word and not by man-made standards. We must be willing to ignore popular opinion, media, government, or other

---

4. W., *Big Book*, 82.
5. Gandhi, "Mahatma Gandhi Quotes."

Part 4: What Does This Mean?

authorities in our culture. This is one of the things that made the first Christians so different from those around them and got the attention of many pagans (though it was not always positive attention). Freedom exists only within those boundaries because the slave of Christ is bound by Acts 5:29: "We must obey God rather than men!" We are responsible for knowing and doing what God tells us in his word. And when we struggle with this, there is always the "1 Cor 10 rule." When something is not forbidden or commanded, it must be either good physically and spiritually for us or for others, or both. The Spirit of Jesus, found in the study of his word, will make us wise in how we relate to others if we are humble enough to be taught by it.

He will teach us how to forgive those who sin against us, and with that, learn how to be free of anger and fear. Practicing forgiveness also makes our relationships work much better. We can learn from him how to work for social change, to "render to Caesar the things that are Caesar's, and to God the things that are God's" (Matt 22:21). In our modern political chaos, the wisdom that comes from understanding how these two kingdoms are meant to work together will help us find our way through the increasing madness of extreme positions.

Jesus can also teach us why it is important to talk to others about our faith. He gives us wisdom about marriage and family, gender, and sexual identity and how best to live within them. This wisdom is not found by those who think they know better than the creator, nor is it found by those who legalistically apply what they want the Bible to say. The slave of Christ is completely humble before the word of their master, seeking to understand him, to do his will not only from the heart but with all their heart. Our radical problem led God to a radical solution. He rescued slaves of sin and death with his cross and made us his slaves. He calls us to a radically different life, but it is a far better life.

The Time Has Come, Again

I. A. H. Combes, in her book on the early Christians' concept of slavery, ends with a thought about using this term "slave of Christ" today: "A language of slavery, even in a culture without a social context of such a metaphor, could enjoy a very valuable rebirth."[6] Since this was the last sentence in her book, she does not elaborate. But I hope that I have made a start, showing why a rebirth of the idea can be very valuable for us today. Not

---

6. Combes, *Metaphor of Slavery*, 172.

as a metaphor, but as a definition, an identity we can not only claim for ourselves and live out in our world but also use as a tool to think with in understanding our world.

The hardest part is that people will not understand the difference between human slavery and belonging to a loving, saving God. They will find it hard not to think as they have been taught to think of slavery in terms of forced labor, legalism, and loss of freedom—mindless drones—instead of freedom from all that is evil, life-destroying, and dehumanizing—a joyous life. If they think God is only an idea, then, of course, they may think we are simply crazy, dangerous religious fanatics who believe in things that simply aren't real. But they might also think that our "imaginary" God does not seem to like them or the things they are passionate about doing. In that case, they may push back. We must remember to counter this with respect, a good deal of listening, compassion, and service. When we talk about our faith it will help to always start with Jesus, not with religion, churches, or even the vague abstraction called Christianity. It is always about Jesus, not about us. We listen. We share. We respond.

Think of the opportunities that living as a slave of Christ will give us to introduce others to the master. We can share why we are thankful for his gift of forgiveness and life, and why we might even serve those who hate us. We can share why we struggle to do what is right in God's eyes. If they think us a bit crazy, we can point out that it is equally crazy to think money will make you happy or to live with a sense that life has no purpose except to "eat, drink, and be merry, for tomorrow we die." How can they live without hope? We can say, "Take heart! There is more!" "There is something better!" "There is an eternal purpose, joy, and peace, but it is found only in belonging to Jesus." Peter tells us how to be ready to say these things. "Have no fear of them, nor be troubled, but in your hearts honor Christ the Lord as holy, always being prepared to make a defense to anyone who asks you for a reason for the hope that is in you; yet do it with gentleness and respect, having a good conscience, so that, when you are slandered, those who revile your good behavior in Christ may be put to shame" (1 Pet 3:14–16).

As our world grows more and more like the world of the first century, it is time for us to understand and live as slaves of Christ, just as Christians did in the first century. It is an idea whose time has come, *again*. Answer our Lord's call to follow him as your master. Do this, as Bonhoeffer said, with your eyes wide open, aware of the "cost of discipleship." But don't lose sight of its promises—all the strength, peace, and wisdom that can belong to those who serve the right master. If you let "slave of Christ" define you, let it guide you, let it be the glasses through which you see yourself and your world, I think you will find that many things in your life will become much better.

Postlude

Holy Sonnets XIV, by John Donne c. 1610[7]

> Batter my heart, three person'd God; for, you
> As yet but knocke, breathe, shine, and seeke to mend;
> That I may rise, and stand, o'erthrow mee, and bend
> Your force, to breake, blowe, burn and make me new.
> I, like an usurpt towne, to'another due,
> Labour to'admit you, but Oh, to no end,
> Reason your viceroy in mee, mee should defend,
> But is captiv'd, and proves weake or untrue.
> Yet dearly 'I love you,' and would be loved faine,
> But am betrothe'd unto your enemie:
> Divorce mee, 'untie, or breake that knot againe,
> Take mee to you, imprison mee, for I
> Except you 'enthrall mee, never shall be free,
> Nor ever chast, except you ravish me.

---

7. Kenner, *Seventeenth Century Poetry*, 63.

Bibliography

Andreau, Jean, and Raymond Descat. *The Slave in Greece and Rome*. Translated by Marion Leopold. Madison: University of Wisconsin Press, 2011.
Barna, George. "American Worldview Inventory 2021." Arizona Christian University Cultural Research Center. https://www.arizonachristian.edu/wp-content/uploads/2021/05/CRC_AWVI2021_Release02_Digital_01_20210427.pdf.
Beard, Mary. *SPQR: A History of Ancient Rome*. New York: Liveright, 2015.
Bonhoeffer, Dietrich. *The Cost of Discipleship*. New York: MacMillan, 1960.
———. *Life Together*. San Francisco: Harper & Row, 1954.
Brown, Francis, et al. *The New Brown, Driver and Briggs Hebrew and English Lexicon of the Old Testament*. Lafayette, IN: Associated Publishers and Authors, 1981.
Browning, Robert. "A Grammarian's Funeral." In *Nelson's English Readings: The Earlier Victorian Period*. Vol. 6. New York: Thomas Nelson, 1930.
Bruce, F. F. *New Testament History*. Garden City, NY: Doubleday, 1980.
Burge, Ryan P. *The Nones: Where They Came From, Who They Are, and Where They Are Going*. Minneapolis: Fortress, 2021.
Byron, John. *Recent Research on Paul and Slavery*. Sheffield, UK: Phoenix, 2008.
Card, Michael. *A Better Freedom: Finding Life as Slaves of Christ*. Downers Grove, IL: InterVarsity, 2009.
Carty, Jay. *Counterattack*. Gresham, OR: Vision House, 1988.
Chesterton, G. K. *The Everlasting Man*. San Francisco: Ignatius, 2008.
———. *Orthodoxy*. New York: Image, 2014.
Cho, Timothy Isaiah. "Slavery, Racial Hierarchy, Charles Hodge, and the Old Presbyterianism." Medium, November 20, 2018. https://timothyisaiahcho.medium.com/slavery-racial-hierarchy-charles-hodge-and-old-school-presbyterianism-8914ef672f6b.
Combes, I. A. H. *The Metaphor of Slavery in the Writings of the Early Church: From the New Testament to the Beginning of the Fifth Century*. Sheffield, UK: Sheffield Academic, 1998.
Crook, John. *Law and Life of Rome*. Ithaca, NY: Cornell University Press, 1967.
Davies, J. G. *The Early Christian Church: A History of Its First Five Centuries*. Grand Rapids: Baker, 1983.
de Wet, Chris L. *Preaching Bondage: John Chrysostom and the Discourse of Slavery in Early Christianity*. Oakland, CA: University of California Press, 2015.
———. *The Unbound God: Slavery and the Formation of Early Christian Thought*. New York: Routledge, 2018.

Bibliography

Dickson, John. *A Doubter's Guide to World Religions*. Grand Rapids: Zondervan, 2022.

Dreher, Rod, *The Benedict Option*. New York: Random House, 2017.

Fluegge, Glenn. "How is Theology a Habitus? Voices from the Past and Why It Matters Today." *Concordia Theological Quarterly* 89:1 (2025) 3–31.

Frankopan, Peter. *The Silk Roads: A New History of the World*. New York: Random House, 2017.

Gandhi, Mahatma. "Mahatma Gandhi Quotes." BrainyQuote. https://www.brainyquote.com/quotes/mahatma_gandhi_150725.

Goodspeed, Edgar. *The Bible: An American Translation*. Chicago: University of Chicago Press, 1951.

Green, Michael. *Evangelism in the Early Church*. Grand Rapids: Eerdmans, 1982.

Grobien, Gifford A. "Spirituales Motus: Sanctification and Spiritual Movements in Believers." *Concordia Theological Quarterly* 87:2 (2023) 330–31.

Harrill, J. Albert. *Slaves in the New Testament: Literary, Social, and Moral Dimensions*. Minneapolis: Fortress, 2006.

Harris, Murray J. *Slave of Christ: A New Testament Metaphor for Total Devotion to Christ*. Downers Grove, IL: InterVarsity, 1999.

Holland, Tom. *Persian Fire: The First World Empire and the Battle for the West*. New York: Anchor, 2007.

Hummel, Horace D. *The Word Becoming Flesh: An Introduction to the Origin, Purpose, and Meaning of the Old Testament*. St. Louis, MO: Concordia, 1979.

Keil, C. F., and F. Delitzsch. *Commentary on the Old Testament*. 10 vols. 1864–1874. Reprint, Grand Rapids: Eerdmans, 1980.

Kenner, Hugh, ed. *Seventeenth Century Poetry: The Schools of Donne and Jonson*. New York: Holt, Rinehart and Winston, 1964.

Kimball, Dan. *They Like Jesus but Not the Church: Insights from Emerging Generations*. Grand Rapids: Zondervan, 2007.

Koehler, Edward. *A Short Explanation of Dr. Martin Luther's Small Catechism*, St. Louis, MO: Concordia, 1971.

Lenski, Richard C. H. *The Interpretation of St. Paul's Epistle to the Romans*. Minneapolis: Augsburg, 1961.

Lewis, C. S. *The Abolition of Man*. New York: HarperCollins, 2001.

———. *The Discarded Image: An Introduction to Medieval and Renaissance Literature*. Cambridge, UK: Cambridge University Press, 2013.

———. *Miracles: How God Intervenes in Nature and Human Affairs*. New York: Macmillan, 1978.

———. *The Problem of Pain*. New York: Macmillan, 1962.

———. *The Weight of Glory and Other Addresses*. New York: Macmillan, 1980.

Luther, Martin. *The Freedom of a Christian*. In *Martin Luther: Selections from His Writings*, edited by John Dillenberger, 42–85. Garden City, NY: Anchor, 1961.

———. *Luther's Small Catechism with Explanation*. St. Louis, MO: Concordia, 2017.

———. "Temporal Authority: To what Extent It Should Be Obeyed." In *Luther's Works*, edited by Helmut Lehmann, 45:75–131. Philadelphia: Muhlenberg, 1962.

Maier, Paul L. *Eusebius' The Church History: A New Translation with Commentary*. Grand Rapids: Kregel, 1999.

Mayer, F. E. *The Religious Bodies of America*. St. Louis, MO: Concordia, 1961.

Mirowsky, John. "Wage Slavery or Creative Work?" *Society of Mental Health* 1.2 (2011): 73–88. https://doi.org/10.1177/2156869311413141.

Bibliography

Pezzo, Federico. "One Word in Four Hundred Words—Otium." *Medicina Narrativa*, December 19, 2023. https://www.medicinanarrativa.eu/otium-2.

Pieper, Francis. *Christian Dogmatics*. Vol. 1. St. Louis, MO: Concordia, 1950.

Plass, Ewald, ed. *What Luther Says: An Anthology*. Vol. 1. St. Louis, MO: Concordia, 1959.

Porter, Joshua. "The Shaker Design Philosophy." http://bokardo.com/archives/the-shaker-design-philosophy/.

Ramelli, Ilaria L. E. *Social Justice and the Legitimacy of Slavery: The Role of Philosophical Asceticism from Ancient Judaism to Late Antiquity*. Oxford, UK: Oxford University Press, 2016.

Ramsay, David. "A Dissertation on the Manner of Acquiring the Character and Privileges of a Citizen of the United States." (1789) In the digital collection *Evans Early American Imprint Collection*. https://name.umdl.umich.edu/N17114.0001.001.

Russell, D. S. *Between the Testaments*. Philadelphia: Fortress, 1981.

Sande, Ken. *The Peacemaker: A Biblical Guide to Resolving Personal Conflict*. Grand Rapids: Baker, 2004.

Scaer, Peter. "At Home in the Body: Lutheran Identity." *Concordia Theological Quarterly* 85:1 (2021) 61–72.

Sherwin-White, A. N. *Roman Society and Roman Law in the New Testament*. Grand Rapids: Baker, 1978.

Sophocles. *Oedipus Tyrannus*. Translated by Luci Berkowitz and T. F. Brunner. New York: Norton, 1970.

Stowe, Harriet Beecher. *Uncle Tom's Cabin*. Ebook. Durham, NC: Duke Classics, 2012.

Strathmann, Herman. "πολίς." In *Theological Dictionary of the New Testament*, translated and edited by G. W. Bromiley, 6:516–35. Grand Rapids: Eerdmans, 1968.

Tappert, Theodore, ed. *The Book of Concord: The Confessions of the Evangelical Lutheran Church*. Philadelphia: Fortress, 1959.

Terry, Milton S. *Biblical Hermeneutics: A Treatise on the Interpretation of the Old and New Testaments*. Grand Rapids: Zondervan, 1981.

Trueman, Carl. *The Rise and Triumph of the Modern Self*. Wheaton, IL: Crossway, 2020.

W., Bill. *Alcoholics Anonymous: The Big Book: The Original 1939 Edition*. Garden City, NY: Dover, 2019.

Wright, Christopher J. H. *An Eye for an Eye: The Place of Old Testament Ethics Today*. Downers Grove, IL: InterVarsity, 1983.

Zimmerli, Walther. "παῖς θεοῦ." In *Theological Dictionary of the New Testament*, translated and edited by G. W. Bromiley, 5:654–77. Grand Rapids: Eerdmans, 1968.

www.ingramcontent.com/pod-product-compliance
Lightning Source LLC
Chambersburg PA
CBHW072137160426
43197CB00012B/2149